I0439827

September 2014

CRITICAL INFRASTRUCTURE PROTECTION

DHS Action Needed to Enhance Integration and Coordination of Vulnerability Assessment Efforts

This report was revised on September 17, 2014, to correct a typographical error on page 19, figure 2.

September 2014

CRITICAL INFRASTRUCTURE PROTECTION

DHS Action Needed to Enhance Integration and Coordination of Vulnerability Assessment Efforts

GAO Highlights

Highlights of GAO-14-507, a report to congressional requesters

Why GAO Did This Study

Damage from natural disasters like Hurricane Sandy in 2012 highlights the vulnerability of the nation's CI. CI includes assets and systems whose destruction would have a debilitating effect on security, national economic security, or national public health or safety. The private sector owns the majority of the nation's CI, and multiple federal entities, including DHS, are involved in assessing its vulnerabilities. These assessments can identify factors that render an asset or facility susceptible to threats and hazards. GAO was asked to review how federal entities assess vulnerabilities.

This report examines the extent to which DHS is positioned to (1) integrate DHS vulnerability assessments to identify priorities, (2) identify duplication and gaps within its coverage, and (3) manage an integrated and coordinated government-wide assessment approach. GAO reviewed CI laws, regulations, data from fiscal years 2011-2013, and other related documentation, as well as interviewed officials at DHS, other agencies, and a private CI association.

What GAO Recommends

GAO recommends that DHS identify the areas assessed for vulnerability most important for integrating and comparing results, establish guidance for DHS offices and components to incorporate these areas into their assessments, ensure that assessment data are consistently collected, and work with other federal entities to develop guidance for what areas to include in vulnerability assessments, among other things. DHS concurred with these recommendations.

View GAO-14-507. For more information, contact Stephen Caldwell at (202) 512-8777 or caldwells@gao.gov.

What GAO Found

During fiscal years 2011 to 2013, various Department of Homeland Security (DHS) offices and components conducted or required thousands of vulnerability assessments of critical infrastructure (CI), but DHS is not positioned to integrate them in order to identify priorities. Although the Homeland Security Act of 2002 and the *National Infrastructure Protection Plan* (NIPP) call for DHS to integrate CI vulnerability assessments to identify priorities, the department cannot do so because of variation in the areas to be assessed for vulnerability included in the various tools and methods used by DHS. GAO analysis of 10 of these assessment tools and methods found that they consistently included some areas, such as perimeter security, but other areas, such as cybersecurity, were not consistently included in the 10 tools and methods. Also, GAO's analysis and discussions with DHS officials showed that DHS's assessments vary in their length and detail of information collected, and DHS has not established guidance on what areas should be included in a vulnerability assessment, such as vulnerabilities to all-hazards as called for in the NIPP. DHS's Office of Infrastructure Protection (IP) has recognized the challenge of having different approaches and has begun to take action to harmonize them. However, of the 10 assessment tools and methods GAO analyzed, IP's harmonization effort includes two voluntary IP assessment tools and none of the other 8 tools and methods GAO analyzed that are used by other DHS offices and components. By reviewing the tools and methods to identify the areas of vulnerability and level of detail that DHS considers necessary, and establishing guidance for DHS offices and components regarding which areas to include in their assessments, DHS would be better positioned to integrate assessments to enable comparisons and determine priorities between and across CI sectors.

DHS offices and components have not consistently captured and maintained data on vulnerability assessment activities in a way that allows DHS to identify potential duplication or overlap in coverage among vulnerability assessment activities they have conducted or required. As a result, DHS is not positioned to track its activities to determine whether its assessment efforts are potentially duplicative or leave gaps among the CI assessed and thereby better ensure effective risk management across the spectrum of assets and systems, as called for by the NIPP. Developing an approach to collect data consistently would facilitate DHS's identification of potential duplication or overlap in CI coverage. Having consistent data would also better position DHS to minimize the fatigue CI owners expressed experiencing from participation in multiple assessments.

DHS is not positioned to manage an integrated and coordinated government-wide approach for assessments as called for in the NIPP because it does not have sufficient information about the assessment tools and methods conducted or offered by federal entities external to DHS with CI responsibilities, such as the Environmental Protection Agency, which oversees critical infrastructure activities related to water and wastewater systems. Consequently, opportunities exist for DHS to work with other federal entities to develop guidance as necessary to ensure consistency. Doing so would better position DHS and other federal entities with CI responsibilities to promote an integrated and coordinated approach for conducting vulnerability assessments of CI, as called for in the Homeland Security Act of 2002, presidential directives, and the NIPP.

_____ **United States Government Accountability Office**

Contents

Tables

Figures

Abbreviations

BASE	Baseline Assessment for Security Enhancements
CFATS	Chemical Facility Anti-Terrorism Standards
CFSR	Critical Facility Security Reviews
CI	critical infrastructure
CREAT	Climate Resilience Evaluation and Awareness Tool
CSAT SVA	Chemical Security Assessment Tool Security Vulnerability Assessment
DHS	Department of Homeland Security
DOE	Department of Energy
DOT	Department of Transportation
EPA	Environmental Protection Agency
FDA	Food and Drug Administration
FERC	Federal Energy Regulatory Commission
FPS	Federal Protective Service
GSA	General Services Administration
IP	Office of Infrastructure Protection
ISC	Interagency Security Committee
ISCD	Infrastructure Security Compliance Division
IST	Infrastructure Survey Tool
JVA	Joint Vulnerability Assessment
MIST	Modified Infrastructure Survey Tool
MTSA	Maritime Transportation Security Act
NIPP	National Infrastructure Protection Plan
NPPD	National Protection and Programs Directorate
NRC	Nuclear Regulatory Commission
PCII	Protected Critical Infrastructure Information
PPD	Presidential Policy Directive
PSA	Protective Security Advisor
PSCD	Protective Security Coordination Division
RRAP	Regional Resilience Assessment Program
SSA	sector-specific agency
SAV	Site Assistance Visit
TSA	Transportation Security Administration
TSARK	TSA Risk Knowledge Center
VAST	Vulnerability Assessment Software Tool
VSAT	Vulnerability Self Assessment Tool

September 15, 2014

The Honorable Michael T. McCaul
Chairman
Committee on Homeland Security
House of Representatives

The Honorable Peter T. King
Chairman
Subcommittee on Counterterrorism and Intelligence
Committee on Homeland Security
House of Representatives

The Honorable Patrick Meehan
Chairman
Subcommittee on Cybersecurity, Infrastructure Protection, and Security
Technologies
Committee on Homeland Security
House of Representatives

In the fall of 2012, the remnants of Hurricane Sandy caused widespread
damage to infrastructure across multiple states and affected millions of
people. Damage included flooding in the nation's financial center that
affected major transportation systems and caused widespread and
prolonged power outages. The damage and resulting chaos disrupted
government and business functions alike, producing cascading effects far
beyond the location of these events. The extensive damage and long
recovery required from disasters like Hurricanes Katrina and Sandy, as
well as the terrorist attacks of September 11, 2001, highlight the
vulnerability of our nation's critical infrastructure (CI) to various hazards
and the importance of CI security and resilience. Critical infrastructure
includes assets and systems, whether physical or virtual, so vital to the
United States that their incapacity or destruction would have a debilitating
impact on security, national economic security, national public health or
safety, or any combination of those matters.[1] Because the private sector
owns the majority of the nation's CI—financial institutions, commercial
facilities, and energy production and transmission facilities, among

---

[1]See 42 U.S.C. § 5195c(e).

others—it is vital that the public and private sectors work together to protect these assets and systems.

The Department of Homeland Security (DHS) was established in 2002 with broad missions including preventing terrorist attacks within the United States; reducing the vulnerability of the United States to terrorism, and assisting in the recovery from attacks that occur within the United States.[2] According to the Homeland Security Act of 2002, as amended, DHS is to, among other things, carry out comprehensive vulnerability assessments of CI; integrate relevant information, analyses, and assessments from within DHS and from CI partners; and use the information collected to identify priorities for protective and support measures.[3] Pursuant to Presidential Policy Directive (PPD)-21, DHS is to coordinate the overall federal effort to promote the security and resilience of the nation's critical infrastructure from all-hazards.[4] DHS issued the National Infrastructure Protection Plan (NIPP) in 2006, to provide the overarching approach for integrating the nation's CI security and resilience activities into a single national effort.[5] The NIPP, which was updated in 2009, and most recently in 2013, sets forth a risk management framework and outlines the roles and responsibilities of DHS with regard to CI security and resilience.[6] The NIPP risk management framework is a

---

[2] See Pub. L. No. 107-296, § 101, 116 Stat. 2135, 2142 (2002).

[3] These responsibilities were assigned by the Homeland Security Act of 2002, as amended, to an Assistant Secretary for Infrastructure Protection. See 6 U.S.C. § 121. The Secretary of Homeland Security delegated those responsibilities to the Under Secretary for the National Protection and Programs Directorate.

[4] Presidential Policy Directive/PPD-21—Critical Infrastructure Security and Resilience (Washington, D.C.: Feb. 12, 2013). PPD-21 defines resilience as the ability of CI to prepare for and adapt to changing conditions and withstand and recover rapidly from disruptions, and is an area that may be included in vulnerability assessments to determine the extent to which CI is prepared to withstand and recover from disruptions such as exposure to a given hazard or incidents arising from the deliberate exploitation of a vulnerability.

[5] DHS, *National Infrastructure Protection Plan* (Washington, D.C.: December 2006). DHS updated the NIPP in January 2009 to include greater emphasis on resiliency. See DHS, *National Infrastructure Protection Plan, Partnering to Enhance Protection and Resiliency* (Washington, D.C.: January 2009). DHS updated the NIPP in December 2013 to emphasize the integration of physical and cybersecurity into the risk management framework. See DHS, *2013 National Infrastructure Protection Plan, Partnering for Critical Infrastructure Security and Resilience* (Washington, D.C.: December 2013).

[6] Broadly defined, risk management is a process that helps policymakers assess risk, strategically allocate finite resources, and take actions under conditions of uncertainty.

planning methodology that outlines the process for setting goals and objectives; identifying assets, systems, and networks; assessing risk based on consequences, vulnerabilities, and threats; implementing protective programs and resiliency strategies; and measuring performance and taking corrective action. Within DHS, the National Protection and Programs Directorate (NPPD) has been delegated the responsibility for the security and resilience of the nation's critical infrastructure, and within NPPD, the Office of Infrastructure Protection (IP) leads and coordinates national programs and policies on critical infrastructure issues.

PPD-21 and the NIPP also call for other federal departments and agencies to play a key role in CI security and resilience activities in their capacity as sector-specific agencies (SSA). An SSA is a federal department or agency responsible for, among other things, security and resilience programs and related activities of designated critical infrastructure sectors, which are logical collections of assets, systems, or networks that provide a common function to the economy or government.[7] There are 16 critical infrastructure sectors, some of which have DHS as their SSA and others that have federal agencies or departments external to DHS as their SSAs. For example, DHS is the exclusive SSA for the commercial facilities and dams sectors, and the Department of Energy (DOE) and the Environmental Protection Agency (EPA) are the exclusive SSAs for the energy and water sectors, respectively. Consistent with the NIPP and PPD-21, DHS also shares SSA responsibilities with the Department of Transportation (DOT) for the transportation sector, and the General Services Administration (GSA) for the government facilities sector.[8] Appendix I shows the 16 sectors and their SSAs.

---

[7]The 2006 NIPP listed 17 critical infrastructure sectors, consistent with Homeland Security Presidential Directive/HSPD-7, which directed DHS to establish uniform policies, approaches, guidelines, and methodologies for integrating federal infrastructure protection and risk management activities within and across critical infrastructure sectors (Washington, D.C.: Dec. 17, 2003). In 2008, DHS established an 18th sector—critical manufacturing. Presidential Policy Directive/PPD-21 revoked HSPD-7 and realigns the 18 sectors into 16 critical infrastructure sectors, and provides that plans developed pursuant to HSPD-7 shall remain in effect until specifically revoked or superseded.

[8]Within DHS, the Coast Guard and the Transportation Security Administration (TSA) have responsibility for the transportation sector, and the Federal Protective Service (FPS) has responsibility for the government facilities sector.

Over the last several years, DHS has taken actions to assess vulnerabilities at CI facilities and within groups of related infrastructure, regions, and systems. According to DHS, a vulnerability assessment is a process for identifying physical features or operational attributes that render an entity, asset, system, network, or geographic area open to exploitation or susceptible to a given hazard that has the potential to harm life, information, operations, the environment, or property.[9] DHS further notes that vulnerability assessments can produce comparable estimates of vulnerability across a variety of hazards or assets, systems, or networks. These assessments include areas that can be assessed for vulnerability (hereinafter referred to as "areas"), such as perimeter security, the presence of a security force, or vulnerabilities to intentional acts, including acts of terrorism.

Some assessments are required by DHS components as part of regulatory regimes. For example, the Coast Guard requires facilities it regulates under the Maritime Transportation Security Act of 2002 (MTSA) to complete assessments as part of their security planning process.[10] However, other assessments are voluntary. For example, within DHS's NPPD, the Protective Security Coordination Division (PSCD) relies on vulnerability assessments that CI owners and operators voluntarily participate in to help identify potential actions to secure CI.[11] SSAs external to DHS also offer vulnerability assessment tools and methods to owners or operators of CI, and these assessments include areas such as resilience management or perimeter security. For example, EPA, the SSA for the water sector, provides a self-assessment tool for the conduct of voluntary security-related assessments at water and wastewater facilities. Given the large number of different agencies, both within and outside of

---

[9]According to the NIPP, vulnerabilities may be associated with physical (e.g., no barriers or alarm systems), cyber (e.g., lack of a firewall), or human (e.g., untrained guards) factors. A vulnerability assessment can be a stand-alone process or part of a full risk assessment and involves the evaluation of specific threats to the asset, system, or network under review to identify areas of weakness that could result in consequences of concern. For the purposes of this report, we use the term "tools and methods" when referring to specific survey questionnaires or tools that DHS offices and components and other federal agencies use in conducting vulnerability assessments or in offering self-assessments to CI owners and operators. These tools and methods contain various areas that can be assessed for vulnerabilities, such as perimeter security, entry controls, and cybersecurity, among others.

[10]See Pub L. No. 107-295, 116 Stat. 2064 (2002).

[11]See app. II for descriptions of DHS vulnerability assessment tools and methods.

DHS, involved in conducting or requiring vulnerability assessments of CI or offering assessments to owners and operators of CI, there is also the potential for duplication, overlap, or fragmentation between and among the various efforts.

As the fiscal pressures facing the nation continue, so too does the need for executive branch agencies and Congress to improve the efficiency and effectiveness of government programs and activities. Given the necessity for federal agencies to maximize the efficiency and effectiveness of their programs and activities, you asked us to examine the various efforts by DHS offices and components and SSAs to conduct or offer vulnerability assessments of CI. This report assesses the extent to which DHS is positioned to

- integrate DHS vulnerability assessments to identify priorities and enable comparisons,
- identify and address duplication and gaps in its vulnerability assessment activities, and
- manage an integrated and coordinated government-wide approach for vulnerability assessment activities.

To address all of our objectives, we reviewed applicable laws, regulations, and directives as well as policies and procedures to identify (1) DHS offices and components with SSA responsibilities for assessing CI and agencies external to DHS with SSA or sector responsibilities and (2) areas to be included in some assessments. We also identified various criteria relevant to these programs, including the Homeland Security Act of 2002, Presidential Policy Directive/PPD-21 and policies and procedures outlined in the NIPP. Furthermore, we applied definitions for fragmentation, overlap, and duplication, as discussed in our past work.[12]

---

[12]In 2010, Congress mandated that we identify programs, agencies, offices, and initiatives with duplicative goals and activities within departments and government-wide and report annually. See GAO, *Opportunities to Reduce Potential Duplication in Government Programs, Save Tax Dollars, and Enhance Revenue*, GAO-11-318SP (Washington, D.C.: Mar. 1, 2011); *2012 Annual Report: Opportunities to Reduce Duplication, Overlap, and Fragmentation, Achieve Savings, and Enhance Revenue*, GAO-12-342SP (Washington, D.C.: Feb. 28, 2012); *2013 Annual Report: Actions Needed to Reduce Fragmentation, Overlap, and Duplication and Achieve Other Financial Benefits*, GAO-13-279SP (Washington, D.C.: Apr. 9, 2013); and *2014 Annual Report: Additional Opportunities to Reduce Fragmentation, Overlap, and Duplication and Achieve Other Financial Benefits*, GAO-14-343SP (Washington, D.C.: Apr. 8, 2014).

GAO-14-507 Vulnerability Assessments

To address our first objective, we met with officials from the DHS offices and components that conduct or require such assessments (PSCD, Infrastructure Security Compliance Division (ISCD), FPS, TSA, and the Coast Guard) in Washington, D.C., to identify potential vulnerability assessment tools and methods for CI performed or offered by these offices and components.[13] We also obtained and analyzed the most recent tools and methods they used to conduct those assessments. On the basis of this preliminary work, we further analyzed 10 of these vulnerability assessment tools and methods that (1) were used or required by a DHS office or component to conduct assessments at individual CI assets or facilities during fiscal years 2011 to 2013, and (2) contained two or more areas to be assessed.[14] We selected this time period to reflect the period in which PSCD had been using its most recent methodology update to its vulnerability assessment tools. We obtained and analyzed data on the number of assessments conducted by each DHS office or component using its respective tools and methods and the number of facilities regulated under MTSA and the Chemical Facility Anti-Terrorism Standards (CFATS). To assess the reliability of the data, we reviewed existing documentation and information about the data systems used to house the data and spoke with or received information from knowledgeable agency officials responsible for the databases about the sources of the data and DHS's quality assurance procedures. While the information in the data sets provided by each office or component was

---

[13]According to the NIPP, risks to critical infrastructure can be assessed in terms of threat (a natural or man-made occurrence, individual, entity, or action that has or indicates the potential to harm life, information, operations, the environment, or property), vulnerability (the physical features or operational attributes that render an entity open to exploitation or susceptible to a given hazard), and consequence (effect of an event, incident, or occurrence). For the purposes of this review, we only considered assessments related to vulnerability.

[14]DHS offices and components also conduct vulnerability assessments or offer other assessments and tools to assess specific areas (i.e., cybersecurity) or systems composed of more than one asset or facility. For the purposes of this review, we did not include these assessments and tools in our analysis because they assessed a specific area or were composite assessments of more than one CI asset or facility. For example, assessments focusing only on one area, such as DHS's Office of Cybersecurity and Communications cybersecurity assessments or the Cybersecurity Capability Maturity Model offered by DHS and DOE, or on more than one asset or facility such as the port-wide Area Maritime Security Assessments required under MTSA, were not included in our analysis. Other tools and methods may have also been used by the offices and components, but they were either discontinued during the period covered by our review or did not facilitate a comparison. For instance, one tool involves video imaging of a facility, rather than an evaluative assessment. For more information on our scope and methodology, see app. III.

sufficiently reliable for the purposes of documenting what assessments had been completed and where, issues with the comparability of information in each data set exist, which are discussed in this report. We compared the various assessment tools and methods to focus on the areas addressed and the scope and comprehensiveness of the topics discussed in each. We also obtained information and interviewed NPPD officials at DHS headquarters regarding their efforts to develop and implement the "single assessment methodology with a strategic integrated approach" (single assessment methodology) for critical infrastructure assessments to determine the project's scope, time frames, and anticipated impact on future assessments both within and external to DHS.[15] We then compared the results of our analysis with the criteria outlined in the Homeland Security Act of 2002; PPD-21; the NIPP; as well as our work on fragmentation, overlap, and duplication.[16]

To address our second objective, we used the data that we obtained from DHS for the period covering fiscal years 2011 to 2013, discussed in objective one above, to analyze the extent to which the same critical infrastructure was assessed by different entities within DHS. To do our analysis, we used a statistical software program and manual data matching to compare data on over 25,000 assessment-related activities conducted and completed using the 10 vulnerability assessment tools and methods for fiscal years 2011 to 2013.[17] We also interviewed DHS field-based officials at selected locations to obtain information on their roles in assessing CI, and the extent to which (1) assets may have received assessment requests by multiple offices or components and (2) assessments may have been canceled because of assets being previously assessed by another DHS office or component. The locations were Anchorage, Alaska; Houston, Texas; Portland, Oregon; Seattle, Washington; and Tampa, Florida, which we selected to provide variety in the types of CI assets assessed and geographic location, among other factors. We also interviewed an official of a national association

---

[15]According to information provided by NPPD officials, NPPD is in the process of developing what is described as a single assessment methodology with a strategic integrated approach, which is intended to integrate various assessment methodologies into a single consolidated assessment methodology for the department and its partners to use in assessing vulnerabilities of critical infrastructure, among other things.

[16]See GAO-11-318SP, GAO-12-342SP, GAO-13-279SP, and GAO-14-343SP.

[17]See app. III for more information on the methodology used to perform this analysis.

representing private sector CI owners and operators within 1 of the 16 sectors to obtain their perspectives on DHS's CI vulnerability assessment activities. Interviews with these officials cannot be generalized to the universe of CI sectors and locations. However, when combined with the information gathered on DHS documentation and program guidance, they provide insights into how the assessment efforts are being carried out in practice. We then compared the results of our analysis with various criteria, including the Homeland Security Act of 2002; PPD-21; the NIPP; as well as our prior work on fragmentation, overlap, and duplication.

To address our third objective, we also reviewed documentation and interviewed officials at federal agencies external to DHS with SSA or sector specific regulatory responsibilities (Departments of Agriculture, Defense, Energy, Health and Human Services, Transportation, and Treasury; Environmental Protection Agency; Federal Energy Regulatory Commission; Food and Drug Administration; General Services Administration; and the Nuclear Regulatory Commission) to inventory their assessment tools and methods.[18] We compared this inventory against one that DHS IP provided of the assessment tools and methods that it was aware SSAs external to DHS provide. Because our scope for this work focused on those CI security-related assessment tools and methods identified by DHS and the SSAs external to DHS, the list we compiled through this work is not necessarily exhaustive and there may be additional tools and methods offered by others that we did not capture as part of our work. However, this information provided insights as to the extent to which assessment tools and methods were being offered or provided by other agencies and departments external to DHS. To understand the requirements in handling and sharing certain critical information collected for some assessments—information designated as Protected Critical Infrastructure Information (PCII)—we interviewed officials in DHS's PCII Program Office and reviewed documentation on

---

[18]See app. I for a list of the sectors and their respective SSAs.

GAO-14-507 Vulnerability Assessments

PCII regulations and requirements.[19] Finally, we compared the results of our work with criteria outlined in the Homeland Security Act of 2002; PPD-21; the NIPP; federal internal control standards; as well as our prior work on fragmentation, overlap, and duplication.[20] Appendix III discusses our scope and methodology in greater detail.

We conducted this performance audit from April 2013 to September 2014 in accordance with generally accepted government auditing standards. Those standards require that we plan and perform the audit to obtain sufficient, appropriate evidence to provide a reasonable basis for our findings and conclusions based on our audit objectives. We believe that the evidence obtained provides a reasonable basis for our findings and conclusions based on our audit objectives.

Background

Various laws and directives guide DHS's role in CI protection, including the Homeland Security Act of 2002, as amended,[21] and more recently,

---

[19]In general, PCII is validated Critical Infrastructure Information (CII)—that is, information not customarily in the public domain and related to the security of critical infrastructure or protected systems—that is voluntarily submitted, directly or indirectly, to DHS for its use regarding the security of critical infrastructure and protected systems, analysis, warning, interdependency study, recovery, reconstitution, or other appropriate purpose. See 6 C.F.R. § 29.2(b), (g). Pursuant to the Critical Infrastructure Information Act of 2002, DHS established the PCII program to institute a means to facilitate the voluntary sharing of critical infrastructure information with the federal government by providing assurances of safeguarding and limited disclosure. See 6 U.S.C. §§ 131-34; see also 6 C.F.R. pt. 29 (implementing the CII Act through the establishment of uniform procedures for the receipt, care, and storage of voluntarily submitted CII). DHS has established a PCII Program Office, which is responsible for, among other things, validating information provided by CI partners as PCII and developing protocols to access and safeguard all that is deemed PCII.

[20]GAO, *Standards for Internal Control in the Federal Government*, GAO/AIMD-00-21.3.1 (Washington, D.C.: Nov. 1, 1999). Internal control is an integral component of an organization's management that provides reasonable assurance that the following objectives are being achieved: effectiveness and efficiency of operations, reliability of financial reporting, and compliance with applicable laws and regulations. These standards, issued pursuant to the requirements of the Federal Managers' Financial Integrity Act of 1982 (FMFIA), provide the overall framework for establishing and maintaining internal control in the federal government.

[21]See generally Pub. L. No. 107-296, 116 Stat. 2135 (2002). Title II of the Homeland Security Act, as amended, primarily addresses the department's responsibilities for critical infrastructure protection.

Presidential Policy Directive/PPD-21.[22] As mentioned previously, according to the Homeland Security Act of 2002, as amended, DHS is to, among other things, carry out comprehensive vulnerability assessments of CI; integrate relevant information, analyses, and assessments from within DHS and from CI partners; and use the information collected to identify priorities for protective and support measures. PPD-21 directs DHS to, among other things, provide strategic guidance, promote a national unity of effort, and coordinate the overall federal effort to promote the security and resilience of the nation's CI. PPD-21 also states that DHS, in carrying out its responsibilities under the Homeland Security Act of 2002, as amended, evaluates national capabilities, opportunities, and challenges in protecting CI; analyzes threats to, vulnerabilities of, and potential consequences from all-hazards on CI; identifies security and resilience functions that are necessary for effective public-private engagement with all CI sectors; integrates and coordinates federal cross-sector security and resilience activities, and identifies and analyzes key interdependencies among CI sectors, among other things.

Related to PPD-21, the NIPP calls for the CI community and associated stakeholders to carry out an integrated approach to (1) identify, deter, detect, disrupt, and prepare for threats and hazards (all-hazards); (2) reduce vulnerabilities of critical assets, systems, and networks; and (3) mitigate the potential consequence to CI from incidents or events that do occur. According to the NIPP, CI partners are to identify risk in a coordinated and comprehensive manner across the CI community; minimize duplication; consider interdependencies; and, as appropriate, share information within the CI community. Furthermore, the NIPP risk management framework is designed to provide flexibility for use in all sectors so that it can be tailored to dissimilar operating environments and apply to all threats and hazards. Specifically, the NIPP states that common definitions, scenarios, assumptions, metrics, and processes can ensure that risk assessments, which include vulnerability assessments, contribute to a shared understanding among CI partners. The NIPP also calls for risk assessments to be documented, reproducible, and defensible to generate results that can contribute to cross-sector risk comparisons for supporting investment, planning, and resource

---

[22]PPD-21—*Critical Infrastructure Security and Resilience* (Washington, D.C.: Feb. 12, 2013).

prioritization decisions.[23] Table 1 provides a description of these core criteria for risk assessments.

Table 1: *National Infrastructure Protection Plan* (NIPP) Core Criteria for Risk Assessments

Criterion	Description
Documented	The methodology and the assessment must clearly document what information is used and how it is synthesized to generate a risk estimate. Any assumptions, weighting factors, and subjective judgments need to be transparent to the user of the methodology, its audience, and others who are expected to use the results. The types of decisions that the risk assessment is designed to support and the timeframe of the assessment (e.g., current conditions versus future operations) should be given.
Reproducible	The methodology must produce comparable, repeatable results, even though assessments of different critical infrastructure and key resources may be performed by different analysts or teams of analysts. It must minimize the number and impact of subjective judgments, leaving policy and value judgments to be applied by decision makers.
Defensible	The risk methodology must logically integrate its components, making appropriate use of the professional disciplines relevant to the analysis, and be free from significant errors or omissions. Uncertainty associated with consequence estimates and confidence in the vulnerability and threat estimates should be communicated.

Source: 2013 N PP Supplemental Tool: Executing a Critical Infrastructure Risk Management Approach. | GAO-14-507

Within DHS, NPPD's IP has overall responsibility for coordinating implementation of the NIPP across the 16 CI sectors, including (1) providing guidance to SSAs and asset owners and operators on protective measures to assist in enhancing the security of infrastructure, and (2) helping state, local, tribal, territorial, and private sector partners develop the capabilities to mitigate vulnerabilities and identifiable risks to the assets.[24] The NIPP also designates other federal agencies, as well as DHS, as SSAs that are responsible for, among other things, coordinating with DHS and other federal departments and agencies and CI owners and operators; providing, supporting, or facilitating technical assistance and consultations for the sector to identify vulnerabilities and help mitigate

---

[23]DHS, *National Infrastructure Protection Plan, Partnering for Critical Infrastructure Security and Resilience.*

[24]A delegation memo to the Under Secretary for NPPD delineates the directorate's roles and responsibilities.

GAO-14-507 Vulnerability Assessments

incidents, as appropriate; and supporting DHS's statutory reporting requirements by providing, on an annual basis, sector specific critical infrastructure information.

Prior GAO Work on Fragmentation, Overlap, and Duplication

In 2010, Congress mandated that we identify programs, agencies, offices, and initiatives with duplicative goals and activities within departments and government-wide and report annually.[25] In March 2011, February 2012, April 2013, and April 2014, we issued our annual reports to Congress in response to this requirement.[26] The annual reports describe areas in which we found evidence of fragmentation, overlap, or duplication among federal programs, including those managed by DHS.[27] Using the framework established in our prior work on addressing fragmentation, overlap, and duplication, we use the following definitions for the purpose of assessing DHS's vulnerability assessment-related efforts:

- Fragmentation occurs when more than one agency (or more than one organization within an agency) is involved in the same broad area of national interest.
- Overlap occurs when multiple programs have similar goals, engage in similar activities or strategies to achieve those goals, or target similar beneficiaries. Overlap may result from statutory or other limitations beyond the agency's control.
- Duplication occurs when two or more agencies or programs are engaging in the same activities or providing the same services to the same beneficiaries.

---

[25]Pub. L. No. 111-139, § 21, 124 Stat. 29 (2010), 31 U.S.C. § 712 Note.

[26]See GAO-11-318SP, GAO-12-342SP, GAO-13-279SP, and GAO-14-343SP.

[27]See GAO, *Department of Homeland Security: Oversight and Coordination of Research and Development Should Be Strengthened*, GAO-12-837 (Washington, D.C.: Sept. 12, 2012), for an example of our work on selected DHS programs we identified as fragmented and overlapping.

DHS Vulnerability Assessments Vary in Content, and DHS Is Not Positioned to Integrate Assessments to Identify Priorities

DHS has conducted or required asset owners and operators to conduct thousands of vulnerability assessments of critical infrastructure using a variety of assessment tools and methods and has taken some initial actions to begin to harmonize some of these tools and methods. However, DHS is not well positioned to integrate relevant assessments to identify priorities for protective and support measures or to support nationwide, comparative risk assessments because the assessment tools and methods used vary in length, detail, and areas assessed. DHS has also not issued guidance to the DHS offices or components involved in these assessments to ensure that the areas that DHS deems most important are captured in their assessment tools and methods.

DHS Offices and Components Have Conducted or Required Thousands of Vulnerability Assessments, Some of Which Are Voluntary

Our analysis of data on 10 DHS vulnerability assessment tools and methods showed that, from October 2010 to September 2013, DHS offices and components collectively conducted or required owners and operators to conduct thousands of assessments of critical infrastructure assets and systems.[28] Specifically, DHS officials representing NPPD, TSA, and the Coast Guard conducted more than 5,300 assessments using eight different assessment tools and methods covering various types of assets and systems. During the same time period, as many as 7,600 asset owners and operators were required to perform self-assessments to comply with two regulatory regimes—MTSA and CFATS—administered by the Coast Guard and an NPPD component—ISCD. Figure 1 shows the number of assessments conducted by DHS offices and components and the approximate number of self-assessments required by ISCD and the Coast Guard under CFATS and MTSA, respectively.

---

[28]During the early stages of our review, NPPD, TSA, and Coast Guard officials identified various assessment tools and methods. We further analyzed these 10 assessment tools and methods because based on our preliminary work, these tools and methods contained two or more areas assessed for vulnerability, such as perimeter security or the presence of a security force.

Figure 1: Critical Infrastructure (CI) Vulnerability Assessments Conducted by Department of Homeland Security (DHS) Offices and Components or CI facilities, Fiscal Years 2011 to 2013

Number of CI vulnerability assessments conducted by DHS office or component	Number of CI vulnerability assessments conducted by facilities
National Protection and Programs Directorate	
Protective Security Coordination Division (PSCD) 3,255[a]	Infrastructure Security Compliance Division (ISCD)-Chemical Facility Anti-Terrorism Standards regulated facilities 3,300 to 4,100[c]
Federal Protective Service (FPS)[b] 1,458[a]	
U.S. Coast Guard	
Office of International and Domestic Port Assessment 93[a]	Office of Port and Facility Activities Maritime Transportation Security Act regulated facilities 2,800 to 3,500[c]
Transportation Security Administration (TSA)	
Office of Law Enforcement 74[a]	
Office of Security Operations/Compliance 349[a]	
Office of Security Operations/Compliance/ Office of Security Policy and Industry Engagement 122[a]	
Total 5,351	6,100 to 7,600

Source: GAO analysis of data and information from DHS PSCD and ISCD, FPS, TSA, and U.S. Coast Guard. | GAO-14-507

[a]This reflects the total actual number of assessments conducted by the office or component during the covered time period.

[b]The Federal Protective Service conducts assessments of facilities owned or leased by the General Services Administration as part of its protection responsibilities.

[c]The number of facilities actively regulated under Maritime Transportation Security Act and Chemical Facility Anti-Terrorism Standards requirements can fluctuate over time because of facilities changing their regulated operations or the types and quantities of chemicals handled, new facilities being built, or older facilities being decommissioned, for example. The numbers presented here represent the approximate number of facilities covered by the regulations at any given time during our period of analysis. Therefore, these are an estimated range of the number of facilities that were required to conduct a vulnerability assessment for DHS to meet the applicable regulatory requirements.

DHS offices and components or asset owners and operators have used various assessment tools and methods, some of which are voluntary, while others are required by law or regulation, to gather information about certain aspects of CI. The 10 assessment tools and methods we analyzed ranged from those used in voluntary vulnerability assessments performed by PSCD field representatives, called Protective Security Advisors (PSA);[29] to the self-assessments required by ISCD and the Coast Guard under the CFATS and MTSA regulatory programs; to various assessments of airports, pipelines, and rail and transit systems, performed by TSA officials.[30] Table 2 lists the 10 types of vulnerability assessment tools and methods we analyzed that were used or required by various offices in NPPD, the Coast Guard, and TSA.

Table 2: Types of Department of Homeland Security (DHS) Critical Infrastructure Vulnerability Assessment Tools and Methods Analyzed

Types of voluntary assessment tools or methods	Types of regulatory or required assessment tools or methods
National Protection and Programs Directorate (NPPD) • Infrastructure Survey Tool (IST) • Site Assistance Visit (SAV)	National Protection and Programs Directorate (NPPD) • Chemical Security Assessment Tool Security Vulnerability Assessment (CSAT SVA) • Modified Infrastructure Survey Tool (MIST)[a]
Transportation Security Administration (TSA) • Baseline Assessment for Security Enhancements (BASE)[b] • Freight Rail Risk Analysis Tool • Pipeline Security Critical Facility Security Reviews (CFSR)	Transportation Security Administration (TSA) • Joint Vulnerability Assessment (JVA)
U.S. Coast Guard • Port Security Assessments	U.S. Coast Guard • Maritime Transportation Security Act (MTSA)-regulated facility vulnerability assessments

Source: GAO analysis of DHS vulnerability assessments. | GAO-14-507

Note: During the early stages of our review, NPPD, TSA, and Coast Guard officials identified various assessment tools and methods. We further analyzed these 10 vulnerability assessment tools and

[29]As of July 2014, DHS has deployed 89 PSAs in all 50 states, Puerto Rico, and the nation's capital region to, among other things, conduct outreach with state and local partners and asset owners and operators who participate in DHS's voluntary CI protection and resiliency efforts.

[30]Pursuant to 49 U.S.C. § 44904, TSA and the Federal Bureau of Investigation (FBI) are to conduct joint threat and vulnerability assessments at each high-risk U.S. airport at least every 3 years. See 49 U.S.C. § 44904(a)-(b). See also Pub. L. No. 104-264, § 310, 110 Stat. 3213, 3253 (1996) (establishing the requirement that the Federal Aviation Administration [FAA] and the FBI conduct joint threat and vulnerability assessments). Pursuant to the Aviation and Transportation Security Act, responsibility for conducting the joint assessments transferred from FAA to TSA. TSA is required to conduct vulnerability assessments on 34 specific passenger airports. In addition to these statutorily required joint vulnerability assessments, TSA conducts joint vulnerability assessments on airports that volunteer to be assessed.

methods because based on our preliminary work, these tools and methods contained two or more areas to be assessed for vulnerability, such as perimeter security or the presence of a security force.

[a]MIST is used by the Federal Protective Service (FPS) to assess federal facilities. FPS is required to perform facility security assessments of federal facilities as part of its protection responsibilities.

[b]Although the BASE does not include an evaluation of specific threats to identify areas of weakness that could result in consequences of concern, we included it in our analysis because it is used to assess vulnerabilities of mass transit systems and infrastructure.

The vulnerability assessment tools and methods DHS offices and components use vary greatly in their length and the detail of information to be collected. For example, NPPD IP's PSCD uses its IST to assess facilities that voluntarily participate, and this tool is used across the spectrum of CI sectors. The IST, which contains more than 100 questions and 1,500 variables, is used to gather information on the security posture of CI, and the results of the IST can inform owners and operators of potential vulnerabilities facing their asset or system. In another example, NPPD IP's ISCD requires owners and operators of facilities that possess, store, or manufacture certain chemicals under CFATS to provide data on their facilities using an online tool so that ISCD can assess the risk posed by covered facilities. This tool, ISCD's Chemical Security Assessment Tool Security Vulnerability Assessment (CSAT SVA), contains more than 100 questions based on how owners respond to an initial set of questions. TSA's Office of Security Operations (OSO) offers or conducts a number of assessments, such as a 205-question assessment of transit systems called the Baseline Assessment for Security Enhancements that contains areas to be assessed for vulnerability, and TSA's 17-question Freight Rail Risk Analysis Tool is used to assess rail bridges. The Coast Guard conducts voluntary assessments as part of its Port Security Assessment Program on 25 port facilities annually to support risk mitigation strategies. The Port Security Assessment can contain anywhere from 16 questions to more than 100 questions per facility in total when considering other stakeholders who are also asked to participate in the assessment. Table 3 shows the minimum number of possible questions for the 10 assessment tools and methods, and the number of pages for each. Appendix II discusses each of these tools and methods and their basis in law or regulation.

Table 3: Length of Department of Homeland Security (DHS) Vulnerability Assessment Tools and Methods (Number of Pages and Questions), by Type

Vulnerability assessment tool or method	DHS office or component	Number of pages	Minimum number of questions
Infrastructure Survey Tool (IST)	National Protection and Programs Directorate (NPPD)	296	More than 100[a]
Site Assistance Visit (SAV)	NPPD	253	More than 100[a]
Chemical Security Assessment Tool Security Vulnerability Assessment (CSAT SVA)	NPPD	107	More than 100[a]
Modified Infrastructure Survey Tool (MIST)	NPPD	165	More than 100[a]
Joint Vulnerability Assessment (JVA)	Transportation Security Administration (TSA)	57[b]	More than 100[a]
Baseline Assessment for Security Enhancements (BASE)	TSA	14	205
Pipeline Security Critical Facility Security Review (CFSR)	TSA	21	166
Freight Rail Risk Analysis Tool	TSA	1	17
Port Security Assessment[c]	Coast Guard	5[d]	16
Maritime Transportation Security Act (MTSA)[e]	Coast Guard	Not applicable	Not applicable

Source: GAO analysis of DHS documents. | GAO-14-507

[a]The number of questions asked varies depending on responses. For example, if a question elicits a "yes" response, additional details may be elicited by the tool, whereas a "no" response may not prompt additional questions.

[b]Approximately nine pages of the assessment are infrastructure specific.

[c]Port Security Assessment activities include eight questionnaires directed to various port facility stakeholders such as local emergency managers and facility owners and operators. Therefore, an individual facility may be asked fewer questions, but in total these eight questionnaires contain more than 100 questions.

[d]According to Coast Guard officials, this reflects the minimum number of pages of the questionnaire templates used to gather initial background and contextual information on an asset or facility before an assessment. During the assessment, the assessment team uses its subject matter expertise and professional judgment to determine what type and how many additional questions to ask.

[e]Neither MTSA nor its implementing regulations prescr be individual questions to be asked; rather, the regulations contain topics that are required to be addressed during the required assessment, such as existing security and safety equipment and response capability to security incidents. See 33 C.F.R. § 105.305.

Assessments Vary, and DHS Has Not Integrated the Assessments or Issued Guidance to Better Ensure Consistency

The assessments conducted or required by DHS offices and components also vary with respect to the areas of vulnerability assessed depending on which DHS office or component conducts or requires the assessment. As a result, it is not clear what areas DHS believes should be included in a comprehensive vulnerability assessment. Moreover DHS has not issued guidance to ensure that the areas it deems most important are captured in assessments conducted or required by its offices and components.

Our analysis showed that DHS vulnerability assessments consistently included some areas that were assessed for vulnerability and included other areas that were not consistently assessed. Specifically, we compared the 10 assessment tools and methods identified in table 3 to determine the extent and consistency of information to which DHS has access for decision making. Our analysis showed that 10 of the 10 assessment tools and methods we analyzed included areas such as "vulnerabilities from intentional acts"—such as terrorism—and "perimeter security" in the assessment. However, 8 of the 10 assessment tools and methods did not include areas such as "vulnerabilities to all-hazards" such as hurricanes or earthquakes. These exclusions are not in alignment with the NIPP, which calls for CI risk management to be inclusive of significant threats and hazards. Of the 10 assessment tools and methods, 8 included "resilience management." With respect to "cybersecurity," 4 of the 10 assessment tools and methods did not include "cybersecurity" even though PPD-21 calls for the Secretary of Homeland Security to identify and prioritize CI, considering both physical and cyber threats. Likewise, Coast Guard regulations under MTSA call for MTSA reviews to include the identification of measures to protect radio and telecommunication equipment, including computer systems and networks, which could include "cybersecurity."[31] However, Coast Guard assessments are among the 4 of 10 assessment tools and methods that do not currently include "cybersecurity."[32] These differences in areas assessed among the various assessment tools and methods could complicate or hinder DHS's ability to (1) integrate relevant assessments in order to identify priorities for protective and support measures and (2)

---

[31]See 33 C.F.R. § 105.305(d)(2)(v).

[32]According to Coast Guard officials, the Coast Guard is in the process of incorporating critical infrastructure cybersecurity into its programs. They also noted that the agency has chartered a work group to identify how cyber will affect its missions and stakeholders and is in the process of developing a strategy for how it will address cybersecurity more broadly.

Figure 2: Comparison of Selected Areas Included in Department of Homeland Security (DHS) Vulnerability Assessment Tools and Methods

Assessment tool or method

Area	National Protection and Programs Directorate				Transportation Security Administration				U.S. Coast Guard	
	Infrastructure Survey Tool	Site Assistance Visit	Chemical Security Assessment Tool / Security Vulnerability Assessment	Modified Infrastructure Survey Tool	Joint Vulnerability Assessment	Baseline Assessment for Security Enhancements	Pipeline Security Critical Facility Security Review	Freight Rail Risk Analysis Tool	Port Security Assessment	Maritime Transportation Security Act
Vulnerabilities to intentional acts	✓	✓	✓	✓	✓	✓	✓	✓	✓	✓
Vulnerabilities to all hazards	✓	✓								
Resilience management	✓	✓	✓			✓	✓	✓	✓	✓
Security force	✓	✓	✓	✓	✓	✓	✓		✓	✓
Perimeter security	✓	✓	✓	✓	✓	✓	✓	✓	✓	✓
Entry controls	✓	✓	✓	✓	✓	✓	✓		✓	✓
Electronic security systems	✓	✓	✓	✓	✓	✓	✓		✓	✓
Utility systems/providers/dependencies identified	✓	✓	✓	✓	✓	✓	✓		✓	✓
Cybersecurity	✓	✓	✓	✓	✓	✓				
Inventory controls/measures	✓	✓	✓	✓		✓	✓			✓

Source: GAO analysis of DHS documents. | GAO-14-507

Note: This analysis is not inclusive of all areas included in the various assessments. We selected these areas because each was included in at least two DHS vulnerability assessment tools or methods. A checkmark indicates that the area was included or mentioned in at least one question in the assessment tool or method. Therefore, a checkmark is not to be considered an indication of how complete, sufficient, or extensive the coverage is for a given area by an assessment tool or method. Other areas exist that may be necessary for an assessment to be considered comprehensive such as questions specific to buildings, in addition to perimeter security, that could render them vulnerable to certain hazards or threats, or questions related to information sharing that could identify vulnerabilities in response and recovery to hazards or threats.

In addition to differences in what areas were included, there were also differences in the detail of information collected for individual areas, making it difficult to determine the extent to which the information collected was comparable and what assumptions or judgments were used while gathering assessment data. These variations could impede DHS's ability to integrate relevant information and use it to identify priorities for protective and support measures regarding terrorist and other threats to homeland security. Specifically, while some components asked open-ended questions such as "describe security personnel," others included drop-down menus or lists of responses to be selected. Collecting data in such different formats or styles could complicate DHS's ability to integrate information from the various assessment tools and methods. We also observed that components used different questions for the same areas assessed. For example, the level of detail explored under "resilience management" varied, with some tools and methods being more complex than others. Specifically, we found that some tools and methods focused on "resilience management" in terms of a backup location or alternative site, while others considered more complex factors—the interconnectedness and interdependencies of CI—such as water supply or electricity reliance, consistent with the NIPP. The following examples show the extent to which some tools and methods varied in the level of detail within areas, differences that could hinder or complicate DHS's ability to integrate and use them to, among other things, support national-level, comparative risk assessments, and resource prioritization.

- Resilience management – PSCD's IST and SAV and TSA's Pipeline Security Critical Facility Security Review (CFSR) each contain questions for this area, but the level of detail of the questions varies.[33] For example, PSCD's IST and SAV contain questions for "resilience management" that focus on, among other things, business continuity,

---

[33]During the course of our review, DHS issued its 2015 Budget-in-Brief, which indicated that SAVs, which were previously conducted as stand-alone assessments or as part of Regional Resiliency Assessment Program (RRAP) activities, will be discontinued in fiscal year 2015. According to DHS officials, the resources formerly utilized for SAVs will be directed toward the expansion of RRAP assessments and enhancement of the IST. The RRAP is an analysis of infrastructure clusters and systems in specific geographic areas or regions. Using the RRAP, DHS examines vulnerabilities, threats, and potential consequences to identify (1) dependencies and interdependencies among the assets that participate in the RRAP, (2) cascading effects resulting from an all-hazards disruption of these assets or the region, (3) characteristics that make the assets and the region resilient, and (4) any resilience gaps that may hinder rapid recovery from disruptions. As a separate initiative, PSCD officials told us they plan to enhance the PSA-conducted ISTs to, among other things, provide written options for consideration, that were previously provided only to SAV participants.

such as details about whether the business continuity plan has procedures for such things as alert and notification to employees, location and relocation procedures, information technology recovery, pandemic response, or reconstitution of normal operations. By contrast, TSA's Pipeline CFSR has "resilience management" questions related to how long it takes to restore emergency service, estimated reconstruction costs, and estimated daily loss of revenue.

- Security force – PSCD's IST prompts the user to provide a greater level of detail than TSA's Freight Rail Risk Analysis Tool. Specifically, the IST contains more than 20 questions related to "security force" and prompts responses on various factors such as training, equipment, and surge capacity. By contrast, the Freight Rail Risk Analysis Tool contains 1 question that focuses on whether employees are present at a given site—but the tool is unclear whether the question is focused on the security force or other employees at the site.

- Cybersecurity – TSA's BASE and ISCD's CSAT SVA each contain questions related to "cybersecurity," but the questions differ in the level of detail to be provided. For example, TSA's BASE contains 7 questions related to cybersecurity strategy, such as whether the agency is aware of and using available resources (e.g., standards, etc.), that could elicit yes or no responses and leave the inclusion of additional information to the discretion of the assessor. By contrast, ISCD's CSAT SVA contains several questions about cybersecurity, including boxes prompting open-ended responses that, depending on how they are answered, could lead to more than 20 different responses listing Cyber Control Systems and other details. Cyber Control Systems deal with controls over aspects of manufacturing facilities, which may include electronic switches that open gates, doors, or valves on pipelines.[34] The CSAT SVA also contains questions related to cyber business systems such as inventory

---

[34]The National Institute of Standards and Technology (NIST) Special Publications (800 Series) was established in 1990 to provide reports on information technology research, guidelines, and outreach efforts in computer security, and its collaborative activities with industry, government, and academic organizations. In addition, in February 2014, in response to Executive Order 13636, which called for the development of a voluntary risk-based Cybersecurity Framework—a set of industry standards and best practices to help organizations manage cybersecurity risks—NIST issued its *Framework for Improving Critical Infrastructure Cybersecurity*, which establishes a common language to address and manage cybersecurity risk in a cost-effective way based on business needs. National Institute of Science and Technology, *Framework for Improving Critical Infrastructure Cybersecurity*, (Gaithersburg, Maryland: February 2014). See Exec. Order No. 13,636, 78 Fed. Reg. 11,739 (Feb. 19, 2013).

management systems and prompts users to provide examples of the systems in place that could result in vulnerabilities to the CI in question.

- Inventory controls/measures – ISCD's CSAT SVA contains more than a dozen "inventory control" questions related to products on site at a given facility, such as the type and quantity of chemicals on site at a regulated facility. In contrast, FPS uses a modified version of PSCD's IST, called the Modified IST (MIST), which contains two "inventory control" questions, and both are related to the retrieval of building keys from employees that no longer work at the site. It does not include an assessment of the extent to which there is an inventory of assets in the building, such as computers or other electronic equipment that could be stolen or targeted during a cyberattack.

Our review and discussions with DHS officials showed that the tools and methods for DHS's vulnerability assessments may be inherently different for a variety of reasons, including different laws, regulations, and policies guiding what areas are included in the assessments and how they are used. Specifically, according to DHS, while some assessments are intended to fulfill regulatory responsibilities, others are intended to help enhance voluntary security and resilience activities. For example, ISCD and the Coast Guard use assessments to help them fulfill their statutory and regulatory responsibilities for securing high-risk chemical facilities and port facilities, respectively.[35] The CFATS rule covers high-risk facilities, which are defined as those that present a high risk of significant adverse consequences for human life or health, national security, or critical economic assets if subjected to terrorist attack, compromise, infiltration, or exploitation.[36] The rule also established 18 risk-based performance standards, such as perimeter security and cyber-security, and facilities are to include in their assessments any existing

---

[35]See Pub. L. No. 109-295, § 550, 120 Stat. 1355, 1388 (2006); 46 U.S.C. § 70102.

[36]6 C.F.R. § 27.105.

GAO-14-507 Vulnerability Assessments

countermeasures that meet the performance standards.[37] Likewise, MTSA regulations specify a required assessment and outline the elements to be included in the assessment.[38] Additionally, FPS, which uses the MIST to perform assessments at General Services Administration–owned or –leased properties and carries out the assessments using criteria based on the Interagency Security Committee's (ISC) Facility Security Level Determinations for Federal Facilities-An ISC Standard.[39] The ISC criteria focus on intentional acts, which is also the focus of the MIST assessment. By contrast, according to DHS officials, PSCD performs assessments—ISTs and SAVs, among others—to help carry out its voluntary CI security and resilience responsibilities across the 16 sectors, consistent with the Homeland Security Act and the NIPP. ISTs and SAVs include questions for the areas "vulnerability to intentional acts" and "vulnerability to all-hazards"

---

[37] 6 C.F.R. § 27.215(a)(3). We previously reported that the CFATS risk assessment process does not currently conform to the NIPP. See GAO, *Critical Infrastructure Protection: DHS Efforts to Assess Chemical Security Risk and Gather Feedback on Facility Outreach Can Be Strengthened*, GAO-13-353 (Washington, D.C.: Apr. 5, 2013). According to the NIPP, risk assessments should identify vulnerabilities, describe all protective measures, and estimate the likelihood of an adversary's success for each attack scenario. Similar to the NIPP, the CFATS rule calls for a review of facilities' security vulnerability assessments as part of the risk-based tiering process, and the vulnerability assessments are to include the identification of potential security vulnerabilities and the existing countermeasures, as well as their level of effectiveness in both reducing identified vulnerabilities and meeting the aforementioned risk-based performance standards. We found that the SVA contains numerous questions aimed at assessing vulnerability and security measures in place, consistent with the CFATS rule. However, although facilities are required to respond to these questions, DHS officials told us that they have opted not to use the data provided because it is "self-reported" data—data that are not validated by DHS—and officials have observed that facility owners and operators tend to either overstate or understate some of the vulnerability information they provide.

[38] Owners or operators of facilities subject to MTSA regulations are required, among other things, to ensure that a facility security risk assessment is conducted. 33 C.F.R. §105.305 establishes the information and analysis requirements for these assessments, such as requiring an "on-scene" survey of the facility.

[39] ISC—an interagency organization led by DHS—is a central forum for standards and guidance that is available for agencies to consult when designing and updating their security programs. ISC's purpose is to enhance the quality and effectiveness of security and the protection of buildings and facilities in the United States occupied by federal employees for nonmilitary activities. Some of the ISC Standards have a status of For Official Use Only and are therefore not publicly available. We have completed a large body of work on ISC Standards and FPS assessments; for example, see GAO, *Homeland Security: Federal Protective Service Continues to Face Challenges with Contract Guards and Risk Assessments at Federal Facilities*, GAO-14-235T (Washington, D.C.: Dec. 17, 2013).

and "cybersecurity" as they are carried out to align with the NIPP, which calls for assessments to consider these three vulnerabilities.

We recognize that various statutes, regulations, directives, and policies can influence what areas are included in some vulnerability assessments offered by DHS offices and components. However, according to the Homeland Security Act of 2002, as amended, DHS is to, among other things, carry out comprehensive vulnerability assessments of CI; integrate relevant information, analysis, and assessments from within DHS and from CI partners; and use the information collected to identify priorities for protective and support measures regarding terrorist and other threats to homeland security. Consistent with the Homeland Security Act, the NIPP calls for improving or modifying existing risk assessment activities, for example, by developing assessments that identify potential vulnerabilities, so that they can be used to support national-level, comparative risk assessments; incident response planning; and resource prioritization. The NIPP also states that assessment activities are to reflect the interconnectedness and interdependencies among CI. Based on our review, given the many different types of vulnerability assessment tools and methods DHS offices and components use, it is unclear what areas DHS believes should be included in a comprehensive vulnerability assessment. Because of these differences, depending on which DHS office or component conducts the assessment of CI, some CI will not receive vulnerability assessments that are as comprehensive as others, which could result in gaps in information about the vulnerabilities facing some CI, such as vulnerabilities to all-hazards or cybersecurity. As a result of their differences and the information gaps, DHS is not in a position to integrate assessments conducted or required by components within DHS to identify priorities for protective and support measures regarding threats to the nation or to support national-level comparative risk assessments.

An official representing DHS's Office of Policy stated that his office is aware of differences in DHS's vulnerability assessments, and that DHS has not established a department-wide policy on how offices and components are to conduct vulnerability assessments or issued guidance on what areas those assessment tools and methods are to include. However, he stated that DHS's Office of Policy has begun to consider how it can better harmonize assessment efforts across DHS. For example, he said this could start with updating DHS's risk lexicon to clarify risk-related terms so that components would have a common language to begin discussions about harmonizing their efforts, including assessments that identify potential vulnerabilities.[40] He also noted that DHS is in the early stages of convening a committee to, among other things, help focus and bring consistency to DHS's risk-related activities. At this stage, this approach appears promising, particularly if aligned with PPD-21 and the NIPP. As discussed earlier, PPD-21 calls for DHS to provide strategic guidance, promote a national unity of effort, and coordinate the overall federal effort to promote the security and resilience of the nation's CI. In addition, the NIPP calls for risk assessments, which include vulnerability assessments, to be documented, reproducible, and defensible to generate results that can contribute to cross-sector risk comparisons for supporting investment, planning, and resource prioritization decisions. Guidance to ensure that the areas it deems most important are captured would better position DHS to support the risk assessments called for by the NIPP.

Likewise, officials representing individual components stated that they have begun to examine how they can harmonize their efforts among particular components with respect to field activities, or assessment areas, such as resilience management. For example, IP officials told us that they recognize the challenges associated with having different assessment activities or approaches, particularly in light of recent budgetary constraints, and have begun to take steps to consolidate IP's voluntary vulnerability assessment tools into a single assessment methodology that can be tailored to meet the needs of CI partners both within IP and across different sectors. According to these officials, this effort builds on the consolidation of the SAV assessment into the IST and replaces and incorporates some IP self-assessment tools that are no

---

[40]DHS, Risk Steering Committee, *DHS Risk Lexicon* (Washington, D.C.: September 2010). DHS developed the risk lexicon to provide a common set of official terms and definitions to ease and improve the communication of risk-related issues for DHS and its partners.

longer offered by DHS.[41] However, as of April 2014, IP officials told us that this effort was limited to some voluntary IP assessments, such as the IST and SAV, and did not extend to other DHS offices and components. Similarly, in April 2014, TSA's Chief Risk Officer told us that TSA plans to take a more comprehensive view of the transportation landscape, the interconnectedness of various transportation modes, and the potential for cascading effects due to disruptions to different modes of transportation.[42] The official also noted that this effort is to align TSA risk-related activities with established DHS guidance and other policies and directives, such as the NIPP and PPD-21.

These efforts are an important step toward harmonizing some DHS assessments, but they are in their early stages and it is unclear whether or how these assessments can be adapted to align with each other. DHS would be better positioned to integrate assessments conducted or required by DHS components and enable comparisons between and across CI sectors by (1) reviewing the vulnerability assessment tools and methods used across DHS, along with policies and guidance related to CI, to identify the most important areas to be assessed and the level of detail that is necessary for DHS to integrate assessments and support national-level comparative risk assessments, and (2) establishing guidance to ensure that the areas DHS determines to be necessary are captured in components' vulnerability assessments. For example, DHS may determine that vulnerabilities to all-hazards and cybersecurity should be incorporated into all DHS vulnerability assessments of CI, as appropriate and consistent with PPD-21. Further, DHS may determine that resilience management should be included in all assessments, to mitigate security gaps that may be occurring at high-priority CI because one or more of the assessment tools and methods used by DHS offices

---

[41]During the course of our review, IP stopped using some self-assessment tools in anticipation of the integration of its assessment efforts into a unified approach and said it will stop using others. For example, IP will no longer use the Constellation/Automated Critical Asset Management System, which is maintained by DHS IP and used by, among others, state and local government officials to gather data on CI, or the Voluntary Chemical Assessment Tool offered by the chemical SSA to chemical facilities that handle quantities of chemicals of interest below thresholds that would render them subject to CFATS regulations. Since IP no longer uses these tools, they were outside the scope of our work. Nonetheless, they provide perspective on the extent to which IP is taking action to consolidate its efforts to assess vulnerabilities.

[42]According to TSA, there are six transportation modes: aviation, freight rail, highway, maritime, mass transit and passenger rail, and pipelines.

and components do not currently consider these areas. This review of assessment tools and methods would also better position DHS to include the same level of detail in each vulnerability assessment, which would, in turn, enable comparisons across assets, systems, and sectors, thereby promoting a framework for a more comprehensive approach to CI security and resilience.

DHS Faces Challenges in Capturing and Sharing Data, Which Limit Its Ability to Identify Duplication and Gaps among Vulnerability Assessment Activities

DHS faces challenges identifying gaps or duplication in coverage among CI vulnerability assessment activities because DHS lacks an approach to consistently capture data on these activities. Further, DHS does not have a process to share data or coordinate assessment activities among the various offices and components.

DHS Data on Assessment Activities Are Not Consistently Captured to Identify and Mitigate Potential Duplication or Overlap

As discussed earlier, DHS offices and components conducted or required at least 10 different types of vulnerability assessments across the 16 CI sectors. We compared data from assessments using the 10 CI assessment tools and methods discussed earlier for the 3-year period covering fiscal years 2011 to 2013 and found that DHS assessment activities were overlapping across some of the sectors, but not others.[43] For example, four of the five offices and components conducting these assessments—the Coast Guard and three NPPD offices (FPS, ISCD, and PSCD)—conducted or required vulnerability assessments involving assets or facilities in at least 8 of the 16 sectors. Furthermore, all five

---

[43]To conduct this analysis, we searched the names of the assets and facilities listed in the assessment records provided by each office and component for key words that might be expected to be found within the respective sectors (i.e., transportation, food, agriculture, commercial, business park, dams, emergency services, water, airport, government, nuclear, defense, health care, financial, communications, chemical, critical manufacturing, information technology, energy, and pipeline, among others). This was supplemented by information from DHS officials, who, after reviewing our analysis, identified additional sectors their assessments or assessment requirements may cover.

offices or components conducted or required vulnerability assessments in two sectors—energy and government facilities sectors. PSCD conducted vulnerability assessments of assets or facilities in all of the sectors. Figure 3 shows the extent to which DHS offices or components conducted or required vulnerability assessments across the various sectors.

Figure 3: Overlap across Sectors where Department of Homeland Security (DHS) Offices and Components Conduct Vulnerability Assessments or Required Asset Owners/Operators to Conduct Vulnerability Assessments, Fiscal Years 2011-2013

Critical infrastructure sector	U.S. Coast Guard[a]	DHS office or component			Transportation Security Administration[b]
		National Protection and Programs Directorate			
		Federal Protective Service	Infrastructure Security Compliance Division	Protective Security Coordination Division	
Chemical	✓		✓	✓	
Commercial facilities	✓	✓	✓	✓	
Communications	✓			✓	
Critical manufacturing	✓c		✓	✓	
Dams	✓			✓	
Emergency services	✓c			✓	
Information technology	✓c		✓	✓	
Nuclear reactors, materials, and waste				✓	
Food and agriculture	✓	✓	✓	✓	
Defense industrial base	✓c	✓	✓	✓	
Energy	✓	✓	✓	✓	✓
Healthcare and public health			✓c	✓	
Financial services	✓	✓		✓	
Water and wastewater systems	✓c	✓		✓	
Government facilities	✓	✓	✓	✓	✓
Transportation systems	✓	✓		✓	✓

Source: GAO analysis of DHS data. | GAO-14-507

[a]The Coast Guard offices conducting or requiring these assessments included the Office of International Domestic Port Assessment and the Office of Port and Facility Activities.

[b]The Transportation Security Administration offices conducting these assessments included the Office of Law Enforcement/Federal Air Marshal Service, the Office of Security Operations, and the Office of Security Policy and Industry Engagement.

[c]The sector was identified by DHS officials as one that their assessments or assessment requirements may also cover.

Given the overlap of DHS's assessments among many of the 16 sectors, we attempted to compare data from each of the five offices and components to determine whether DHS had conducted or required vulnerability assessments at the same asset or system within those sectors. However, we were unable to conduct this comparison because of differences in the way data about these activities were captured and maintained in various systems. To determine this, we used a statistical software program and manual data matching to compare data on assessments conducted and completed across the 10 types of vulnerability assessment tools and methods for fiscal years 2011 to 2013. Using the data available, we compared over 25,000 records of assessment-related activities based on name and location, as no unique numeric identifiers were available.[44] Our analysis showed that the various data sets DHS offices and components used did not share common formats or defined data standards that would enable us to identify matches across sets. For example, across the sets of data from the various offices and components, we found that asset names and addresses generally were not entered in a standardized way or were not available in some cases. Regarding the latter, one IP division was unable to readily provide the street addresses of facilities it assessed as part of the data set it provided to us, a fact that required us to take additional steps to obtain the asset addresses using the component's web portal. In addition, some records showed assets that were listed at the same address in more than one DHS data set but did not have names that matched. Similarly, some company names appeared to be the same or similar on multiple DHS data sets but were listed at different street addresses, on different streets, or had post office boxes instead of physical addresses. In some cases, company or asset names were missing altogether.

Officials representing various DHS offices and components acknowledged they have encountered challenges with the consistency of assessment data across offices and components. They stated that DHS-wide interoperability standards do not exist for them to follow in recording their assessment activities that would facilitate consistency and enable comparisons among the different data sets. For example, a senior official with NPPD's ISCD involved in implementing CFATS requirements told us that ISCD has attempted to match data on facilities covered by CFATS with data from other DHS components, such as the Coast Guard, to identify potential duplication and verify claimed exemptions by owners or

---

[44]See app. III for more information on the methodology used to perform this analysis.

operators of MTSA-regulated facilities, but noted that the process is challenging and resource intensive.[45] The official attributed this to the fact that there is no uniform or coordinated system within DHS to assign individual facilities unique identifying numbers. As a result, data, such as those provided by the Coast Guard for facilities covered by the MTSA, must be manually reviewed to identify potential matches. The official stated that while this was a resource-intensive task, it was important to complete in order to avoid duplication of efforts as well as verify that facilities are appropriately covered under one regulatory program or another.

The lack of common data standards and requirements also inhibits DHS's ability to mitigate the negative effects of federal fatigue—a factor that could impede DHS's ability to garner the participation of CI owners and operators in its voluntary assessment activities. During our review, the Coast Guard, PSCD, and TSA field personnel we contacted reported observing what they called federal fatigue, or a perceived weariness among CI owners and operators who had been repeatedly approached or required by multiple federal agencies and DHS offices and components to participate in or complete assessments. One official who handles security issues for an association representing owners and operators of CI expressed concerns about his members' level of fatigue. Specifically, he shared observations that DHS offices and components do not appear to effectively coordinate with one another on assessment-related activities to share or utilize information and data that have already been gathered by one of them. The official also noted that, from the association's perspective, the requests and invitations to participate in assessments have exceeded what is necessary to develop relevant and useful information, and information is being collected in a way that is not the best use of the owners' and operators' time. As figure 4 illustrates, depending on a given asset or facility's operations, infrastructure, and location, an owner or operator could be asked or required to participate in multiple separate vulnerability assessments.

---

[45]CFATS does not apply to facilities that are regulated by the Coast Guard under MTSA. See 6 C.F.R. § 27.110(b).

Figure 4: Example of a Critical Infrastructure (CI) Asset or Facility Potentially Subject to Multiple Assessment Efforts by Department of Homeland Security (DHS) Offices and Components

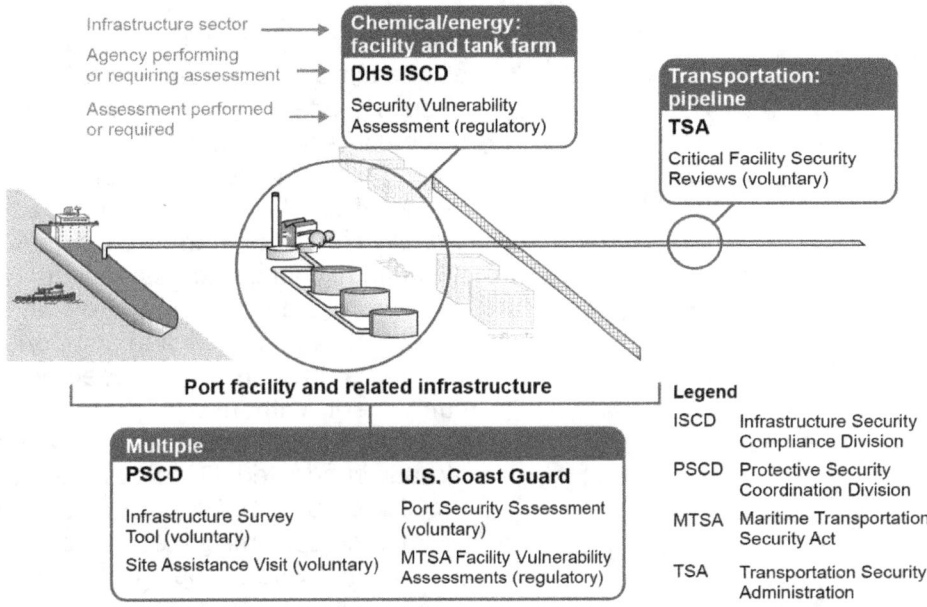

Source: GAO analysis of DHS data. | GAO-14-507

Note: Under CFATS implementing regulations, CFATS would not apply to facilities that are regulated by the Coast Guard under MTSA. See 6 C.F.R. § 27.110(b).

DHS officials expressed concern that this "fatigue" may diminish future cooperation from asset owners and operators. Of the PSAs that we surveyed as part of a prior review regarding their assessment activities, over half of the PSAs reported receiving declinations "often" or "sometimes" by CI owners and operators to requests to participate in a voluntary assessment because their asset was already subject to governmental regulation or inspection.[46] Having common data standards would better position DHS offices and components to minimize this fatigue, and the resulting declines in CI owner and operator participation, by making it easier for DHS offices and components to use each other's data to determine what CI assets or facilities may have been already

---

[46]This survey was conducted as part of our review of PSCD's effort to provide voluntary surveys or vulnerability assessments of CI. See GAO, *Critical Infrastructure Protection: DHS Could Better Manage Security Surveys and Vulnerability Assessments*, GAO-12-378 (Washington, D.C.: May 31, 2012).

GAO-14-507 Vulnerability Assessments

visited or assessed by another office or component. They could then plan their assessment efforts and outreach accordingly to minimize the potential for making multiple visits to the same assets or facilities.

Absent consistent, standardized data on the names and addresses of assets already assessed, DHS is not fully positioned to track its activities to ensure effective risk management across the spectrum of assets and systems as called for by the NIPP. According to the NIPP, managing risk, among other things, entails efficient information exchange through defined data standards and requirements, including an information-sharing environment that has common data requirements and information flow and exchange across entities. However, the lack of consistent, standardized data on the names and addresses of assets already assessed by its offices and components inhibits DHS's ability to identify whether a given asset has been previously assessed by one office or component. Without consistent, standardized data, DHS is not positioned to readily identify potential duplication or overlap among assessments already conducted. Developing an approach to ensure that data gathered on CI assets and systems, such as the names and addresses of the assets and systems assessed, are consistently collected and maintained across DHS would help facilitate the identification of potential duplication or overlap in CI coverage.

There are some approaches DHS could further leverage that it currently has under way. For example, in May 2012, we reported that because of inconsistencies among databases, DHS IP was not positioned to track the extent to which vulnerability assessments were performed at high-priority CI.[47] At that time, DHS IP officials acknowledged that the data did not match and had begun to take actions to improve the collection and organization of the data such as assigning unique identifiers to each asset in the databases used to match or identify the assets for which assessments had been conducted. This is one approach that DHS could consider in determining how to ensure that CI data collected throughout the department are captured in such a way that they are consistent.

Another effort currently under way to enhance the consistency and use of facility- or asset-related information is being led by the Chemical Facility Safety and Security Working Group. Established by Executive Order

---

[47]GAO-12-378.

13650 and composed of representatives from DHS; EPA; and the Departments of Justice, Agriculture, Labor, and Transportation, the working group was directed to identify ways to improve coordination with state and local partners; enhance federal agency coordination and information sharing; modernize policies, regulations, and standards; and work with stakeholders to identify best practices.[48] In May 2014, the working group issued a report on its progress to date, findings and lessons learned, and next steps. As with our findings on the assessment data of DHS offices and components, the working group reported that the individual data sets used and maintained by the various federal agencies involved in chemical facility safety and security had differing formats that made it difficult to identify what facilities identified by one agency might be known by others. In its report, the working group stated that to make coordination and communication among federal agencies more effective, agencies must establish a common data terminology and provide common identifiers for each facility. Toward this end, the working group reported that it planned to, among other things, establish a dedicated cross-agency team of experts to begin work on developing a common facility identifier and data terminology as well as take interim steps to exchange relevant data among all working group members and begin the longer-term process of developing a centralized single data entry portal and data standards. Given the similarities of the challenges the working group identified with the data on facilities with those we identified with the data DHS offices and components have on their assessments of CI, the steps the working group is taking to address these challenges may offer a potential approach that DHS could consider using as well for its data on assessments.

---

[48]On August 1, 2013, the President issued Executive Order 13650–*Improving Chemical Facility Safety and Security*, which was intended to improve chemical facility safety and security in coordination with owners and operators. Exec. Order No. 13,650, 78 Fed. Reg. 48,029 (Aug. 1, 2013).

Lack of Processes for Sharing Data and Coordinating Assessment Activities Can Also Hinder DHS's Ability to Identify Potential Duplication and Gaps in Coverage

In addition to the lack of consistent data on assessments, according to officials at DHS offices and components we contacted, DHS also currently lacks a department-wide process to facilitate data sharing, as appropriate, among the various offices and components that either conduct vulnerability assessments or require assessments on the part of CI owners and operators. Within DHS, various data systems are used by different components to maintain their assessment-related data, but there is no process among the offices and components for sharing the CI data for assessments they conduct, as appropriate. For example, IP has a system called IP Gateway which stores the results of surveys and assessments conducted by its PSCD personnel, while TSA has a separate system called the TSA Risk Knowledge (TSARK) Center that serves as a centralized online repository of TSA's transportation security risk information.[49] However, access to each others' systems is limited or restricted, and there is no other mechanism that consolidates and maintains basic information on the assessment activities of each office or component such as the names and addresses of assets assessed.

Not having access to or a process for sharing information on the assessments can affect DHS offices' and components' ability to identify potential overlap or duplication in their assessment activities. For example, according to TSA officials, for fiscal year 2013, TSA developed nationwide work plans to conduct assessments of a number of highway-related CI assets such as tunnels and bridges. However, only after initiating the first set of assessments and reaching out to the owners or operators of CI assets did TSA learn that the assets had been previously assessed by a different office, NPPD's PSCD. Because these assets had been previously assessed, TSA subsequently cancelled all of its nationwide highway-related-CI assessments planned for that year. A TSA official in the field noted that if the assessments had proceeded, they may have resulted in duplicating previously completed efforts. The field TSA

---

[49]The IP Gateway, formerly known as the Link Encrypted Network System (LENS), hosts IP's facility database, which records, among other things, IP's assessments and other interactions with facilities. The IP Gateway portal is restricted and allows authorized users to obtain, post, and exchange information and access common resources, particularly critical infrastructure information, including security survey data. The TSARK is for TSA personnel and allows multiple TSA offices, divisions and sections to share and access risk information for strategic, operational, and tactical purposes. TSA personnel may extract and share TSARK information with non-TSA offices and personnel on an as-needed basis with consent of the originating TSA program office from which the information was provided. TSA is not contemplating external engagements that provide system access until a fully operational system is built.

official also noted that if officials had access to consistent identifying data, such as the names and addresses of the assets on assessments other DHS offices and components completed, they would be better positioned to plan their assessments accordingly to avoid duplication. Consequently, even if consistent data standards and requirements were in place, the lack of a process for facilitating the sharing of assessment data among offices and components can hinder DHS's ability to analyze what facilities have or have not been assessed because officials using one set of data are not readily able to access and compare the data of other offices and components.

As with the sharing of assessment data, DHS also lacks a department-wide process to facilitate coordination among the various offices and components that conduct vulnerability assessments or require assessments on the part of owners and operators. The NIPP calls for standardized processes to promote integration and coordination of information sharing through, among other things, jointly developed standard operating procedures. However, DHS officials stated that they generally rely on field-based personnel to inform their counterparts at other offices and components about planned assessment activities and share information as needed on what assets may have already been assessed. For example, PSCD officials stated that they send e-mail notifications to partners such as SSAs advising them of planned assessments being conducted by PSAs in the field. They added that PSAs may also inform and invite other partners in their localities to participate in these assessments, if the owner and operator of the asset being assessed concurs. Regarding the latter, PSAs may also alert their DHS counterparts depending on assets covered and their areas of responsibility. Likewise, Coast Guard officials reported that locally based area maritime security committee meetings provide a forum for Coast Guard field personnel to share information about planned and completed assessment-related activities with other DHS components, as needed.[50] However, absent these field-based coordination or sharing activities, it is

---

[50]The area maritime security committees are authorized by section 102 of MTSA, as codified at 46 U.S.C. § 70112(a)(2) and implemented at 33 C.F.R. §§ 103.300-103.310. Typically composed of members from federal, state, and local law enforcement agencies; maritime industry and labor organizations; and other port stakeholders, these committees are responsible for, among other things, identifying critical infrastructure and operations, identifying risks, and providing advice to the Coast Guard for developing the associated area maritime security plan.

unclear whether all facilities in a particular geographic area or sector are covered.

We recognize that DHS field officials play an important role in coordinating vulnerability assessment efforts. However, the lack of a department-wide process for sharing data, as appropriate, and coordinating assessment activities also places DHS at risk of not being able to readily identify potential duplication or gaps in coverage that could leave CI vulnerable to terrorist attacks or all-hazards events. For example, after CFATS took effect in 2007, ISCD officials asked PSCD to stop having PSAs conduct voluntary assessments at CFATS-regulated chemical facilities to reduce potential confusion about DHS authority over chemical facility security and to avoid overlapping assessments. In response, PSCD reduced the number of ISTs and SAVs conducted in the chemical sector. However, one former ISCD official noted that without direct and continuous coordination between PSCD and ISCD on what facilities are being assessed or regulated by each division, this could create a gap in assessment coverage between CFATS-regulated facilities and facilities that could have participated in PSCD assessments given that the number of CFATS-regulated facilities can fluctuate over time.[51] As mentioned previously, according to the NIPP, managing risk entails efficient information exchange through, among other things, an information flow and exchange across entities. Without processes for DHS offices and components to share data and coordinate with each other in their CI vulnerability assessment activities, DHS cannot provide reasonable assurance that it can identify potential overlap, duplication, or gaps in coverage that could ultimately affect DHS's ability to work with its partners to enhance national CI security and resilience, consistent with the NIPP.

---

[51]The number of facilities actively regulated under the Chemical Facility Anti-Terrorism Standards requirements can fluctuate over time because of facilities changing their regulated operations or the types and quantities of chemicals handled, new facilities being built, or older facilities being decommissioned, for example.

DHS Has Insufficient Information to Implement an Integrated and Coordinated Approach for CI Assessments with Other Federal Agencies

Similar to our finding on DHS not being well positioned to integrate its office and component assessments, DHS is also not positioned to manage an integrated and coordinated government-wide approach for CI vulnerability assessment activities as called for by the NIPP because it does not have sufficient information about the various assessment tools and methods used or offered by other federal agencies with CI responsibilities. In September 2013 we asked DHS IP officials to identify vulnerability assessment tools and methods used or offered by SSAs and other federal agencies external to DHS. DHS officials identified 13 assessment tools and methods using a combination of DHS officials' knowledge and familiarity with the sectors, consultation with some SSA officials, and research.[52] After receiving this information from DHS, we contacted the SSAs and other federal agencies to discuss the tools and methods DHS identified. Of the 13 tools and methods identified by DHS, 7 were no longer being used or supported. The SSAs also reported offering 2 additional assessment tools that DHS did not identify.[53] Further, for 1 of the 13 tools and methods, officials with the agency that DHS identified as providing the tool said that their agency had not developed or offered the tool as DHS had asserted. DHS officials told us the list they provided was a snapshot at a given point in time, and they generally do not track these assessment tools and methods as an ongoing part of their operations. According to DHS IP officials, sector specific vulnerability assessment tools and methods offered by SSAs and agencies external to DHS were, in general, provided for the sector partners' benefit at the discretion of the SSA. Table 4 compares information about the various assessment tools and methods that DHS and SSAs external to DHS or other federal agencies with CI responsibilities identified. Appendix V provides additional information about the tools and methods.

---

[52]Other than DOE, SSAs external to DHS do not generally conduct vulnerability assessments of individual assets or facilities; rather, they offer self-assessment tools. According to U.S. Department of Agriculture (USDA) and Food and Drug Administration (FDA) officials, while they do not conduct assessments of individual assets or facilities, they do conduct assessments of supply chains. For example, USDA's Food Safety and Inspection Service (FSIS), pursuant to Homeland Security Presidential Directive 9, conducts vulnerability assessments of the FSIS-regulated commodity supply chains (e.g., meat, poultry, and processed egg products) which are reviewed every 2 years and updated as appropriate. FDA officials stated that they also conduct vulnerability assessments of the food supply chain for products under FDA's regulatory authority.

[53]Officials with the Department of Energy's National Nuclear Security Administration (NNSA) identified additional "performance based" assessments they conduct of their own assets or facilities using modeling or simulation, but we did not include them in our scope because these assessments are not conducted or offered to external CI.

Table 4: Critical Infrastructure Vulnerability Assessment Tools and Methods Offered by Sector-Specific Agencies (SSA) or Agencies External to the Department of Homeland Security (DHS)

Vulnerability assessment tool or method	Department or agency[a]	Sector tool or method is intended for use in	Self-assessment tool or on-site assessment	Tool or method identified by DHS	Tool or method identified by SSA or agency	Tool or method no longer available
Access Delay Knowledge-Based System (ADKBS)	Department of Energy (DOE)	Nuclear	Self-assessment	✓	✓	✓
Adversary Time-Line Analysis System (ATLAS)	DOE	Nuclear	Self-assessment	✓	✓	
Analytic System and Software for Evaluating Safeguards and Security (ASSESS)	DOE	Nuclear	Self-assessment	✓	✓	✓
Climate Resilience Evaluation and Awareness Tool (CREAT)	Environmental Protection Agency (EPA)	Water	Self-assessment		✓	
Dam Assessment Matrix for Security and Vulnerability Risk (DAMSVR)	Federal Energy Regulatory Commission (FERC)	Dams	Self-assessment	✓	✓	
Estimate of Adversary Sequence Interruption (EASI)	DOE	Nuclear	Self-assessment	✓	✓	✓
Radiological Voluntary Security Enhancements	DOE[b]	Nuclear	On-site	✓	✓	
Research and Test Reactors Voluntary Security Enhancement Program	DOE[b]	Nuclear	On-site	✓	✓	
Risk Assessment Methodology for Critical Infrastructures (RAM-CI)	DOE	Various	Self-assessment	✓	✓	✓
Risk Assessment Method-Property Analysis and Ranking Tool (RAMPART)	General Services Administration (GSA)[c]	Government	Self-assessment	✓	✓	✓
Risk Assessment Methodology for Water Utilities (RAM-W)	DOE	Water	Self-assessment	✓	✓	✓
Systematic Analysis of Vulnerability to Intrusion (SAVI)	DOE	Nuclear	Self-assessment	✓	✓	✓
Vulnerability Assessment Software Tool (VAST)	Food and Drug Administration (FDA) and Department of Agriculture (USDA)	Food and agriculture	Self-assessment		✓	
Vulnerability Integrated Security Assessment (VISA)	Nuclear Regulatory Commission (NRC)[d]	Nuclear	Self-assessment	✓		
Vulnerability Self Assessment Tool (VSAT)	EPA	Water	Self-assessment	✓	✓	

Sources: GAO analysis of DHS, DOE, EPA, FDA, FERC, GSA, and USDA data. | GAO-14-507

^aDepartment or agency DHS identified as providing or managing the assessment tool or method. For those tools and methods that DHS did not identify, this denotes the name of the department or agency that identified them.

^bAssessment is carried out by DOE's National Nuclear Security Administration (NNSA) under the Global Threat Reduction Initiative. NNSA began operations in 2000 as a separately organized agency within DOE, responsible for the management and security of the nation's nuclear weapons, nuclear nonproliferation, and naval reactor programs.

^cAccording to GSA officials, RAMPART is a legacy risk tool that was developed by GSA in the late 1990s. The security module in RAMPART has been inactive since fiscal year 2012, but GSA currently uses the tool for environmental and fire safety purposes.

^dWhile DHS identified NRC as providing the tool, NRC reported that DHS incorrectly identified the NRC as providing the VISA methodology. Specifically, the NRC noted that the VISA is a privately-developed tool that is referenced in NRC guidance as an acceptable method by which to conduct security self-assessments, but the NRC does not require its use or provide the tool.

A review of information about three of the tools—two offered by EPA and one offered by FDA and the Department of Agriculture—showed that they contained some areas that were similar to those covered in vulnerability assessments conducted or required by DHS offices and components. However, they also contained differences. For example:

- EPA's Climate Resilience Evaluation and Awareness Tool is a specialized tool intended to help drinking water and wastewater utility owners evaluate and address risks to their utilities from climate change. Like some of the assessments offered by DHS, it focuses on resilience management. However, it does not consider vulnerabilities to intentional acts or cybersecurity, and according to EPA officials, is designed only for climate threats, as opposed to threats from terrorism. EPA developed another tool, described below, to serve as the sector's all-hazards risk assessment tool.
- EPA's Vulnerability Self Assessment Tool is intended to be used by owners and operators of water sector infrastructure to assess both terrorist and natural hazard risks to their systems. Like some of the assessments used by DHS, it includes areas such as cybersecurity, perimeter security, and entry controls. According to EPA officials, this tool was recently upgraded and now includes resiliency metrics.
- FDA's and the Department of Agriculture's Vulnerability Assessment Software Tool is a self-assessment tool that is intended to enable users to assess vulnerabilities of food industry-related infrastructure to intentional attack.[54] Like some of the assessments offered by DHS offices or components, this tool includes areas related to perimeter

---

[54]Two versions of the tool (manufacturing or agriculture) may be utilized depending on the component of the supply chain being assessed.

security, security force, and entry controls. However, it does not consider other areas such as all-hazards vulnerabilities or cybersecurity.

DHS's limited awareness of the various assessment tools and methods that SSAs and other agencies external to DHS offer or no longer offered, and the differences between the assessment tools and methods with respect to content indicates that DHS has not established a fully integrated and coordinated approach as called for by the NIPP, PPD-21, and the Homeland Security Act of 2002. The NIPP states that managing risks to critical infrastructure, including efforts to identify and reduce vulnerabilities, requires an integrated approach across the CI community, which includes federal departments and agencies, such as the SSAs. As discussed previously, the NIPP also calls for risk assessments, which include vulnerability assessments, to be documented, reproducible, and defensible to generate results that can contribute to cross-sector risk comparisons for supporting investment, planning, and resource prioritization decisions. PPD-21 calls for DHS to provide strategic guidance, a national unity of effort, and coordinate the overall federal effort to promote the security and resilience of the nation's CI. In addition, PPD-21 further states that DHS is responsible for conducting comprehensive assessments of the vulnerabilities of the nation's critical infrastructure in coordination with the SSAs and other entities with CI protection responsibilities. However, the lack of a fully integrated and coordinated approach and strategic guidance for managing security-related vulnerability assessments across the CI partnership, to include SSAs and other federal agencies, would, at a minimum, create inefficiencies. This would hinder DHS's ability to integrate assessments from other SSAs to prioritize actions, as called for by the Homeland Security Act of 2002, and enable national-level, comparative risk assessments, as called for by the NIPP. As a result, opportunities exist for DHS and SSAs and other federal agencies with CI responsibilities to work together to advance an integrated and coordinated approach to comprehensive vulnerability assessment activities.

Standards for Internal Control in the Federal Government states that management should have the operational data and information needed to determine whether a program is meeting its goals. Working with SSAs and other federal agencies that have CI security responsibilities to identify key CI security-related assessment tools and methods used or offered by SSAs and other federal agencies external to DHS with CI responsibilities, and then analyzing the tools and methods to determine the areas assessed for vulnerability that they capture, would better position DHS and SSAs to manage risks to CI more comprehensively. Moreover, developing and providing guidance for what areas should be included in vulnerability assessments of CI that DHS, SSAs, and other CI partners can use in an integrated and coordinated manner, among and across sectors, where appropriate, would be consistent with PPD-21 and the NIPP and would also support the risk assessments called for by the NIPP. This would help better ensure assessments are being done consistently across the sectors going forward. Using such an approach would also assist DHS in its efforts to help secure CI because DHS field officials, such as PSAs, and owners and operators of CI assets that have done self-assessments, would have a common frame of reference for discussing security and resilience.

Moving forward, one potential approach for achieving these results would entail using the initiatives discussed earlier in this report that DHS already has under way. Specifically, DHS could explore the feasibility of leveraging IP's single assessment methodology to consolidate its assessment tools and methods and those of the SSAs within DHS to also work with the SSAs and other federal agencies with CI responsibilities outside DHS. This approach could help integrate and coordinate the assessment tools and methods being offered by DHS and the SSAs and other federal agencies external to DHS. Under such a framework, DHS could work with SSAs and other federal agencies with CI responsibilities to identify what assessment tools and methods are being offered, review their content, develop guidance as necessary to ensure consistency, and incorporate them into its approach. The approach could then serve as a centralized portal or repository of assessments for all sectors, not just those for which DHS is the SSA. With such consistency, additional efficiencies could be realized as the results or input from previously completed self-assessments or on-site assessments of facilities could be used, as available, to complete or inform another assessment. For example, a PSA attempting to conduct an IST or SAV on a facility that has already completed a self-assessment would save time and resources by not collecting that information again, and instead focus on verifying it and collecting other information as needed.

According to the director responsible for implementation of IP's single assessment methodology, while his team has considered the assessment tools and methods offered by DHS for incorporation into the approach, the team has not yet considered whether the tools and methods offered by external SSAs could also be incorporated. Nevertheless, an approach to review and consider other assessment activities would also be consistent with actions taken within IP's ISCD wherein officials told us they identified and reviewed existing vulnerability assessment content when developing the SVA to be used to implement CFATS. Specifically, according to a senior ISCD official, CFATS officials reviewed various vulnerability self-assessment tools, including those offered by external SSAs, to determine their content. Likewise, conducting a comprehensive review of the assessment tools and methods provided by SSAs and other federal agencies would enable DHS to better understand the content of the tools and methods and better position DHS and SSAs to promote an integrated and coordinated approach for such assessments.

Another potential framework for DHS to follow in working with SSAs and other federal agencies with CI responsibilities, to guide the content and use of assessment tools and methods, is that of the aforementioned Chemical Facility Safety and Security Working Group. According to a May 2014 status report issued by the working group, the group developed a standard operating procedure, among other things, to help foster a unified approach among the various federal departments and agencies in their efforts to improve the safety and security of chemical facilities. Although the efforts of the working group are focused on regulatory regimes, the outcomes and results of this initiative may provide valuable insights into ways DHS, SSAs, and other agencies can coordinate to help ensure the comprehensiveness of the various assessment tools and methods being used to assess the vulnerabilities of the nation's CI.

Conclusions

While some DHS offices and components have begun to harmonize their vulnerability assessment efforts as called for in PPD-21 and the NIPP, these efforts are in their early stages. Further, DHS is not well positioned to integrate relevant assessments to identify priorities for protective and support measures or to support nationwide, comparative risk assessments as called for by the Homeland Security Act of 2002 and the NIPP. DHS could take additional actions to enhance the comprehensiveness of vulnerability assessments as well as foster a comprehensive approach for CI vulnerability assessment tools and methods used or offered by the federal government. By determining what areas are necessary to include for comprehensive vulnerability assessments and issuing guidance for components to follow, DHS could better ensure that (1) the areas called for by policies and guidance are included in all assessments conducted or required by DHS offices and components, as appropriate, and (2) a similar level of detail, as appropriate, is included in each assessment, which would enable comparisons across assets and sectors. This would better position DHS and its security partners to carry out an integrated approach to risk management, as called for by the Homeland Security Act and the NIPP. In addition, establishing an approach for recording and maintaining data on vulnerability assessments in a consistent manner would enhance the ability of DHS offices and components to minimize duplication of and gaps in information, as well as reduce federal fatigue among CI owners and operators. Further, developing and implementing ways that data can be shared, as appropriate, and coordination facilitated across DHS could also help minimize duplication or gaps in assessment coverage. Moreover, by taking steps to identify the CI security-related assessment tools and methods used or offered by SSAs and other federal agencies external to DHS with CI responsibilities, analyzing them to identify the areas included to assess vulnerability, and working with these SSAs and other federal agencies to develop guidance on what areas to include in vulnerability assessments, DHS would be better positioned to lead a fully integrated and coordinated approach for conducting vulnerability assessments of CI.

Recommendations for Executive Action

Within DHS, to promote efficiency and harmonize the various assessments to advance security and resilience across the spectrum of CI in a manner consistent with the Homeland Security Act of 2002, PPD-21, and the NIPP, we recommend that the Secretary of Homeland Security direct the Under Secretary for the National Protection and Programs Directorate work with other DHS offices and components to take the following three actions:

- review DHS's vulnerability assessments to identify the most important areas to be assessed, consistent with PPD-21 and the NIPP, and determine the areas and level of detail that are necessary for DHS to integrate assessments and enable comparisons, and establish guidance for DHS offices and components to ensure that these areas and level of detail are included, as appropriate, in their assessments;
- develop an approach to ensure that vulnerability data gathered on CI assets and systems are consistently collected and maintained across DHS to facilitate the identification of potential duplication and gaps in CI coverage; and
- develop and implement ways that DHS can facilitate data sharing and coordination of vulnerability assessments to minimize the risk of potential duplication or gaps in coverage.

Regarding SSAs and other federal departments or agencies external to DHS with CI security-related responsibilities that offer or conduct vulnerability assessment tools and methods and building on our recommendation that DHS review its own vulnerability assessments, we recommend that the Secretary of Homeland Security direct the Under Secretary for the National Protection and Programs Directorate work with SSAs and other federal agencies that have CI security responsibilities to take the following three actions:

- identify key CI security-related assessment tools and methods used or offered by SSAs and other federal agencies;
- analyze the key CI security-related assessment tools and methods offered by SSAs and other federal agencies to determine the areas they capture; and
- develop and provide guidance for what areas should be included in vulnerability assessments of CI that can be used by DHS, SSAs, and other CI partners in an integrated and coordinated manner, among and across sectors, where appropriate.

Agency Comments and Our Evaluation

We provided a draft of this report for review and comment to the Department of Health and Human Services (HHS), DHS, DOE, EPA, FERC, GSA, NRC, and USDA. EPA, GSA, and USDA declined to provide comments on our draft report. DHS, DOE, and NRC provided written comments, which are summarized below and reproduced in appendixes VI, VII, and VIII, respectively. In its written comments, DHS concurred with all six recommendations in the report and described actions under way or planned to address them. In addition, DHS, FERC, and HHS also provided technical comments, which were incorporated as appropriate.

Regarding our first three recommendations to DHS, to work together internally to (1) identify the most important areas of vulnerability to be assessed, determine the level of detail necessary to integrate and compare them, and establish guidance to ensure that these areas are included, as appropriate, in the assessments; (2) ensure the consistency of data collected and maintained; and (3) share assessment data and coordinate to minimize potential duplication or gaps in coverage, DHS indicated it planned to take steps that appear to be responsive to our recommendations. For example, DHS noted that it plans to build upon various ongoing initiatives such as NPPD IP's single assessment methodology, IP Gateway, and supplemental guides to the NIPP. In addition, DHS stated that a sub-Interagency Policy Committee of the National Security Council (NSC) is taking steps to identify what policies and guidance are needed to support the identification of information that could be shared across the CI protection community. DHS anticipates this guidance will be issued later this year, and will provide departments and agencies with a common approach to CI data and information. DHS estimates that these various actions will be completed by June 2015, and if implemented effectively, they should address the intent of our recommendations.

Regarding our other three recommendations, concerning the external integration and coordination DHS has with SSAs and other federal agencies with CI protection responsibilities, DHS stated that it plans to take a variety of actions to address our recommendations, including: having NPPD IP lead an inventory survey of the security-related assessment tools and methods the 16 SSAs use to assess CI vulnerabilities, utilizing the inventory data to assess the methodologies and areas covered by each tool, and continuing to refine guidance as necessary such as that provided in the NIPP "Supplemental Tool: Implementing a Risk Management Approach." While these are positive steps, there are additional federal departments and agencies, such as FERC, that are not SSAs but are nonetheless involved in CI security-related activities and may also provide assessment tools and methods. DHS should include these federal departments and agencies as it addresses our recommendations to better ensure that the inventory of assessment tools and methods and any related guidance DHS develops or refines is comprehensive across federal assessments. DHS also noted that while it does not have authority to require inclusion of specific characteristics in vulnerability assessments conducted by other departments and agencies, it can work to promote consistency across assessments to ensure that data are comparable. DHS estimates that two of the three recommendations will be completed by August 2015 and for the other recommendation, regarding analyzing key CI security-related assessment tools and methods, DHS reports that the implementation date is to be determined. If DHS's proposed actions are implemented effectively, they should address the intent of our recommendations.

DOE's written comments did not comment on whether it agreed or disagreed with any of our recommendations, but outline some additional information for consideration. Specifically, DOE stated that the energy sector has its own vulnerabilities, risk acceptance tolerance, and threat mitigation methods and therefore stated that a "one size fits all" approach for vulnerability assessments of CI was not appropriate and that some flexibility must be built in to assess CI. DOE also noted that developing and managing a large database comes at a cost to government and asset owners. We recognize that differences exist between sectors and that a standard uniform assessment across all sectors that does not permit flexibilities is not necessary or appropriate. However, to carry out vulnerability assessments of CI in a manner consistent with the Homeland Security Act, PPD-21, and the NIPP, a minimal level of consistency in the assessments' content is needed, which as our analysis showed, does not currently exist. Thus, we recommended that DHS review the tools and methods to identify the areas and level of detail that are necessary to meet a minimal level of consistency and establish guidance accordingly. Once this minimum, or baseline, is met, it may be appropriate for DHS offices and components and other federal agencies to further tailor the assessments to the needs of their respective sectors. In regard to a database, we do not call for a database, only that DHS develop and implement ways to facilitate data sharing, which could simply be a matter of ensuring that each office or component's data are entered consistently so that they can be readily shared and used as necessary. We defer to DHS to determine what would be the most appropriate and cost-effective way to achieve this. DOE also noted that our report did not address such topics as information sharing between DHS and SSAs, assessments conducted by the private sector, various tools or efforts related to cybersecurity, and the overlap in assessment activities by DHS within the energy sector. We recognize that these are related issues; however, they were outside the scope of our work. Where appropriate, we added additional contextual information in our report.

NRC provided a technical comment in writing and asked that this information be incorporated as an appendix (see app. VIII). We made these revisions as appropriate.

We are sending copies of this report to the Secretary of Homeland Security, the Under Secretary for the National Protection Programs Directorate, and other interested parties. In addition, the report will be available at no charge on the GAO website at http://www.gao.gov.

If you or your staff have questions about this report, please contact me at (202) 512-8777 or caldwells@gao.gov. Contact points for our Offices of Congressional Relations and Public Affairs may be found on the last page of this report. Key contributors to this report are listed in appendix XI.

Stephen L. Caldwell
Director, Homeland Security and Justice Issues

Appendix I: Critical Infrastructure Sectors and Sector-Specific Agencies

This appendix provides information on the 16 critical infrastructure (CI) sectors and the federal agencies responsible for sector security. Presidential Policy Directive/(PPD)-21 and the *National Infrastructure Protection Plan* (NIPP) outline the roles and responsibilities of the Department of Homeland Security (DHS) and its partners—including other federal agencies. Within this framework, DHS is responsible for leading and coordinating the overall national effort to enhance security and resilience of the 16 CI sectors. PPD-21 and the NIPP assign responsibility for critical infrastructure sectors to sector-specific agencies (SSA).[1] As an SSA, DHS has direct responsibility for leading, integrating, and coordinating efforts of sector partners to protect 10 of the 16 CI sectors. The remaining 6 sectors are coordinated by seven other federal agencies. Table 5 lists the SSAs and their sectors.

---

[1]Issued on February 12, 2013, PPD-21, *Critical Infrastructure Security and Resilience* purports to refine and clarify critical infrastructure--related functions, roles, and responsibilities across the federal government, and enhance the overall coordination and collaboration, among other things. Pursuant to Homeland Security Presidential Directive/HSPD-7 and the *National Infrastructure Protection Plan*, DHS had established 18 critical infrastructure sectors. PPD-21 subsequently revoked HSPD-7, and incorporated 2 of the sectors into existing sectors, thereby reducing the number of critical infrastructure sectors from 18 to 16. Plans developed pursuant to HSPD-7, however, remain in effect until specifically revoked or superseded.

Table 5: Critical Infrastructure Sectors and Sector-Specific Agencies (SSA)

Critical infrastructure sector	SSA(s)[a]
Food and agriculture	Department of Agriculture[b] and the Food and Drug Administration[c]
Defense industrial base[d]	Department of Defense
Energy[e]	Department of Energy
Health care and public health	Department of Health and Human Services
Government facilities	Department of Homeland Security and the General Services Administration[f]
Financial services	Department of the Treasury
Transportation systems	Department of Homeland Security and the Department of Transportation[g]
Water and wastewater systems[h]	Environmental Protection Agency
Commercial facilities Critical manufacturing Emergency services Nuclear reactors, materials, and waste Dams Chemical Information technology Communications	Department of Homeland Security

Source: Presidential Policy Directive/PPD-21. | GAO-14-507

[a]Presidential Policy Directive/PPD-21, released in February 2013, identifies 16 critical infrastructure sectors and designates associated federal SSAs. In some cases co-SSAs are designated where those departments share the roles and responsibilities of the SSA.

[b]The Department of Agriculture is responsible for agriculture and food (meat, poultry, and egg products).

[c]The Food and Drug Administration is the Department of Health and Human Services component responsible for food other than meat, poultry, and egg products and serves as the co-SSA.

[d]Nothing in the NIPP impairs or otherwise affects the authority of the Secretary of Defense over the Department of Defense, including the chain of command for military forces from the President as Commander in Chief, to the Secretary of Defense, to the commanders of military forces, or military command and control procedures.

[e]The energy sector includes the production, refining, storage, and distribution of oil, gas, and electric power, except for commercial nuclear power facilities.

[f]Presidential Policy Directive/PPD-21 establishes the General Services Administration as co-SSA with the Department of Homeland Security (DHS) for the government facilities sector. Within DHS, the Federal Protective Service is the responsible component.

[g]Presidential Policy Directive/PPD-21 establishes the Department of Transportation as co-SSA with the Department of Homeland Security (DHS) for the transportation systems sector. Within DHS, the U.S. Coast Guard and the Transportation Security Administration are the responsible components.

[h]The water sector includes drinking water.

Appendix II: Descriptions of Department of Homeland Security Vulnerability Assessment Tools and Methods

This appendix provides information on the Department of Homeland Security (DHS) vulnerability assessment tools and methods we analyzed that were used during fiscal years 2011 to 2013. We selected this time period to reflect the period in which the DHS National Protection and Programs Directorate (NPPD) Office of Infrastructure Protection's Protective Security Coordination Division (PSCD) had been using its most recent methodology update to its vulnerability assessment tools. We also used PSCD as a base because (1) PSCD was the only DHS component that conducted vulnerability assessments in all sectors during the time period and (2) DHS has designated NPPD as the lead component for government-wide critical infrastructure security and resilience. Table 6 shows that DHS offices and components offer a number of assessments that contain various areas, such as addressing all-hazards or focusing on terrorism. As discussed in the report, DHS vulnerability assessments may be conducted to meet the requirements of various laws and directives, and can be regulatory or voluntary. For example, the Coast Guard conducts regulatory activities, as well as voluntary assessments, whereas PSCD offers only voluntary assessments.

Table 6: Descriptions of Department of Homeland Security (DHS) Vulnerability Assessment Tools and Methods

DHS office or component	Assessment tool or method	Description of tool or method
Protective Security Coordination Division (PSCD)	Infrastructure Survey Tool (IST)	ISTs consist of voluntary assessments conducted by Protective Security Advisors (PSA)[a] that gather information on an asset's current security posture and overall security awareness, and assess more than 1,500 variables covering six components—information sharing, security management, security force, protective measures, physical security, or dependencies—as well as 42 more specific subcomponents within those areas, such as specific types of fences, gates, or access controls, among others, which can inform asset owners and operators of potential vulnerabilities they face.
	Site Assistance Visit (SAV)	SAVs consist of an IST and also identify security and resilience gaps and provide options for consideration to mitigate these identified gaps. SAVs are generally on-site and asset-specific and are conducted at the request of owners and operators. The results of SAVs are used to produce a report that includes options for consideration to increase an asset's ability to detect and prevent terrorist attacks and mitigation options that address the identified vulnerabilities of the asset.
Federal Protective Service (FPS)	Modified Infrastructure Survey Tool (MIST)	MIST is a vulnerability assessment based on the IST assessment that has been modified to meet specific FPS criteria. FPS policy dictates that all FPS-protected facilities are subject to recurring assessments based on the Interagency Security Committee's (ISC) *Facility Security Level Determinations for Federal Facilities-An ISC Standard.*

DHS office or component	Assessment tool or method	Description of tool or method
Infrastructure Security Compliance Division (ISCD)	Chemical Facility Anti-Terrorism Standards (CFATS) Security Vulnerability Assessment (SVA)	ISCD requires certain chemical facilities to self-report vulnerability and other information through the Chemical Security Assessment Tool (CSAT) SVA, after which ISCD is to conduct inspections of CFATS-regulated facilities. The SVA contains a number of questions aimed at identifying facility vulnerability and security measures in place. These include questions about the accessibility of the facility to an attacker, the capability of the security force to respond to an attack, and security controls related to potential cyber attacks.
Transportation Security Administration (TSA)	Baseline Assessment for Security Enhancements (BASE)	TSA's BASE program assessment is composed of 205 questions for reviewing a transit systems security posture. According to TSA officials, BASE efforts are not vulnerability assessments but are system-wide reviews of security management, such as security plans, training, personnel management, and processes and procedures in place for working with responders during an incident. The BASE program seeks to identify program gaps or weaknesses and develop best practices applicable to all passenger rail systems.
	Freight Rail Risk Analysis Tool	TSA's Freight Rail Risk Analysis Tool assessments began in fiscal year 2009 focusing on high priority tunnels and bridges based on an industry-provided list of assets.
	Joint Vulnerability Assessment (JVA)	TSA and the Federal Bureau of Investigation (FBI) are to conduct joint threat and vulnerability assessments at each high-risk U.S. airport at least every 3 years. See 49 U.S.C. § 44904(a)-(b). See also Pub. L. No. 104-264, § 310, 110 Stat. 3213, 3253 (1996) (establishing the requirement that the Federal Aviation Administration [FAA] and the FBI conduct joint threat and vulnerability assessments). Pursuant to the Aviation and Transportation Security Act, responsibility for conducting the joint assessments transferred from FAA to TSA. Airports not identified as one of the 34 high-risk airports may receive a JVA through a voluntary request, as a host of a National Special Security Event, or at the direction of TSA senior leadership. The JVA assesses all aspects of an airport's security and operations, in areas such as its perimeter, airport services, airport operations, terminal, and infrastructure systems.
	Critical Facility Security Review (CFSR)	CFSRs are a walkthrough of a pipeline facility that includes asking a common list of questions, discussions with asset owners and operators including corporate executives and security advisers, reviews of plans to protect the pipeline assets, and the adoption of established security guidelines by the assets. Twelve to 18 months following the CFSR, TSA follows up with facility operators to determine if pipeline owners and operators have adopted the established security guidelines and recommendations suggested during the CFSR.[b]

DHS office or component	Assessment tool or method	Description of tool or method
United States Coast Guard	Maritime Transportation Security Act (MTSA)-regulated facility vulnerability assessments	MTSA and its implementing regulations require owners and operators of maritime facilities to conduct security assessments that identify their security vulnerabilities for use in developing security plans to mitigate these vulnerabilities that are valid for 5 years.[c] The Security and Accountability For Every Port Act of 2006 (SAFE Port Act), among other things, amended MTSA to direct the Coast Guard to verify the effectiveness of each facility security plan periodically, but not less than two times per year, at least one of which shall be an inspection of the facility that is conducted without notice to the facility.[d]
	Port Security Assessment	According to Coast Guard officials, the Coast Guard's Office of International and Domestic Port Security Assessment conducts voluntary vulnerability assessments on 25 port facilities annually at five port locations. These efforts are to support risk mitigation strategies. The Port Security Assessments focus on specific threats from intentional acts and assess the prevention, mitigation, and response capabilities of the given facilities. Observations made during Port Security Assessments are non-regulatory and considered no-fault for participants.

Source: GAO analysis of DHS documents and interviews with DHS officials. | GAO-14-507

[a]As of July 2014, PSCD has deployed 89 PSAs in 50 states and Puerto Rico, with deployment locations based on population density and major concentrations of CI. In these locations, PSAs are to act as the link between state, local, tribal, and territorial organizations and DHS infrastructure mission partners in the private sector and are to assist with ongoing state and local CI security efforts. PSAs are also to support the development of the national risk picture by conducting assessments at the nation's high-priority CI. In addition, PSAs are to share vulnerability information and protective measures suggestions with local partners and asset owners and operators, as appropriate.

[b]During the course of our review, TSA officials told us that TSA has the authority promulgate regulations compelling asset owners and operators to participate in these voluntary efforts. The Implementing Recommendations of the 9/11 Commission Act provided that if DHS determines that regulations are appropriate, DHS or the Department of Transportation must promulgate regulations and carry out necessary inspection and enforcement actions. 6 U.S.C. § 1207(d). However, at this time, DHS has not determined that regulations are appropriate and does not plan to impose regulatory requirements.

[c]33 C.F.R. §§ 105.300-.310.

[d]Pub. L. No. 109-347, § 103, 120 Stat. 1884, 1888 (codified at 46 U.S.C. § 70103(c)(4)(D)) The act stipulated that this inspection requirement was subject to the availability of appropriations.

Appendix III: Scope and Methodology

This appendix provides details of our scope and methodology to answer each objective. For all objectives, we reviewed applicable laws, regulations, and directives as well as policies and procedures and our prior reports to identify the Department of Homeland Security (DHS) offices and components with responsibilities for assessing critical infrastructure (CI) and agencies external to DHS with sector-specific agency (SSA) or sector responsibilities, and to identify some common areas identified by policy or regulations to be included in some assessments.[1] We also identified various criteria relevant to these programs and compared the results of our analyses with these criteria, including the Homeland Security Act of 2002, the Presidential Policy Directive/PPD-21, and policies and procedures outlined in the National Infrastructure Protection Plan (NIPP).[2] For each objective, we also compared the results of our analyses and interviews against definitions for fragmentation, overlap, and duplication, as identified in our previous work, to assess the extent to which these assessments were targeted to the same CI or offered the same services to CI.[3]

To address our first objective on the extent to which DHS is positioned to integrate DHS vulnerability assessments to identify priorities and enable comparisons, we reviewed applicable laws, regulations, and directives as well as DHS policies and procedures to identify DHS offices and components with SSA responsibilities for assessing CI, and to identify some common areas identified by policy or regulations to be included in some assessments. In so doing, we identified potential vulnerability assessments performed by the National Protection and Programs Directorate (NPPD), including the Office of Infrastructure Protection's (IP) Protective Security Coordination Division (PSCD) and Infrastructure

---

[1] For a list of prior GAO reports on CI protection and resilience, see the Related GAO Products list at the end of this report.

[2] DHS, *National Infrastructure Protection Plan, Partnering to Enhance Protection and Resilience.*

[3] See GAO, *Opportunities to Reduce Potential Duplication in Government Programs, Save Tax Dollars, and Enhance Revenue,* GAO-11-318SP (Washington, D.C.: Mar. 1, 2011); *2012 Annual Report: Opportunities to Reduce Duplication, Overlap, and Fragmentation, Achieve Savings, and Enhance Revenue,* GAO-12-342SP (Washington, D.C.: Feb. 28, 2012); *2013 Annual Report: Actions Needed to Reduce Fragmentation, Overlap, and Duplication and Achieve Other Financial Benefits,* GAO-13-279SP (Washington, D.C.: Apr. 9, 2013); and *2014 Annual Report: Additional Opportunities to Reduce Fragmentation, Overlap, and Duplication and Achieve Other Financial Benefits,* GAO-14-343SP (Washington, D.C.: Apr. 8, 2014).

Security Compliance Division (ISCD), and the Federal Protective Service (FPS), as well as the Transportation Security Administration (TSA) and the Coast Guard. Among these assessments, we analyzed the assessment tools and methods that DHS or owners and operators applied at individual assets or facilities across the 16 CI sectors that appeared to focus on some common areas. These tools and methods were identified by DHS and, on the basis of our preliminary work, we further analyzed 10 vulnerability assessment tools and methods that (1) were used or required by a DHS office or component to conduct assessments at individual CI assets or facilities during fiscal years 2011 to 2013, and (2) contained two or more areas.[4] We then interviewed DHS officials in Washington, D.C., responsible for administering these programs to identify the key vulnerability assessments of CI conducted by PSCD, ISCD, FPS, TSA, and the Coast Guard. We obtained and compared the most recent tools, surveys, and questionnaires used by them in conducting their assessments to identify key areas assessed and determine the extent to which these offices and components cover similar areas in their assessments, to position DHS to identify priorities and make comparisons. We obtained information and interviewed NPPD officials at DHS headquarters regarding their efforts to develop and implement the single assessment methodology for critical infrastructure assessments to determine the project's scope, time frames, and anticipated impact on

---

[4]DHS offices and components also conduct assessments or offer other assessment tools and methods to assess specific areas or systems composed of more than one asset or facility. For example, NPPD's Office of Cyber Security & Communications (CS&C) offers cybersecurity-focused assessments such as CS&C's Cyber Resilience Review (CRR) and the Cyber Security Evaluation Tool (CSET®). Within TSA, consistent with direction provided in law, the agency implemented Cargo Supply Chain Risk Assessments, which were assessments of entire supply chains composed of multiple facilities and were to be conducted one time in response to the mandate. See Pub. L. No. 110-28, 121 Stat. 112, 140-41 (2007) (providing that the $80 million appropriated for air cargo shall be used to complete air cargo vulnerability assessments for all Category X airports, among other purposes). According to TSA officials, TSA has continued the efforts on a voluntary basis to reach additional partners. Coast Guard regulations to implement MTSA implementing regulations also require that port-wide area maritime security assessments be conducted to examine the threats and vulnerabilities to activities, operations, and infrastructure critical to a port and the consequences of a successful terrorist attack on the critical activities, operations, and infrastructure at the port. 33 C.F.R. §§ 103.400-.410. We did not include these assessment tools and methods in our review because they assessed a specific area or were assessments of more than one CI asset or facility. Other assessment tools and methods may have also been used by components, but they were either discontinued during the period covered by our review or did not facilitate a comparison. For instance, one tool involves video imaging of a facility, rather than an evaluative assessment.

future assessments both within and external to DHS.[5] We also obtained and analyzed data on the number of vulnerability assessments conducted by PSCD, ISCD, FPS, TSA, and the Coast Guard and the number of facilities regulated under the Chemical Facility Anti-Terrorism Standards (CFATS) and Maritime Transportation Security Act (MTSA) during fiscal years 2011 to 2013. As some of the assessment tools and methods have changed over time, to avoid having to analyze multiple versions of the same tool or method, we selected this time frame to reflect the period in which PSCD had been using the most recent version of its vulnerability assessment tools. We used PSCD as a base because (1) PSCD was the only DHS component that conducted vulnerability assessments in all sectors during the time period and (2) DHS has designated NPPD, in which PSCD resides, as the lead component for government-wide critical infrastructure security and resilience. To assess the reliability of the data, we reviewed documentation and information about the various systems used to house the data and spoke with or received information from knowledgeable agency officials responsible for the databases about the agency processes for the collection and maintenance of the data and DHS's quality assurance procedures. While the information in the data sets provided by each office or component was sufficiently reliable for the purposes of documenting what assessments had been completed and for our analyses, issues with the comparability of information in each data set exist, which are discussed in this report.

To address our second objective on the extent to which DHS is positioned to identify and address overlap and gaps in its vulnerability assessment activities, we used the data we obtained from the various DHS offices and components on the records of CI assessments they completed and the regulatory programs they oversaw requiring that owners or operators of regulated CI complete assessments.[6] For self-conducted assessments by owners and operators of MTSA-regulated facilities, we asked the Coast Guard to provide the names, addresses, and dates of all annual

---

[5]According to information provided by NPPD officials, NPPD is in the process of developing what is described as a single assessment methodology with a strategic integrated approach, which is intended to integrate the various assessment methodologies into a single consolidated assessment methodology for the department and its partners to use in assessing vulnerabilities of critical infrastructure, among other things.

[6]These regulatory programs include the Chemical Facility Anti-Terrorism Standards, overseen by the Infrastructure Security Compliance Division (ISCD) and the Coast Guard regulations implementing MTSA. 6 C.F.R. pt. 27; 33 C.F.R. pt. 105.

compliance exams and security spot checks it conducted at regulated facilities during our period of analysis.[7] To identify potential overlap across sectors where DHS offices and components conduct vulnerability assessments or required asset owners and operators to conduct assessments, we searched the names of the assets and facilities listed in the assessment records provided by each office and component for key words that might be expected to be found within the respective sectors (i.e., transportation, food, agriculture, commercial, business park, dams, emergency services, water, airport, government, nuclear, defense, health care, financial, communications, chemical, critical manufacturing, information technology, energy, and pipeline, among others). For example, if the name of a facility or a facility address included the word "dam," that facility was attributed to the dams sector. This was supplemented by information from DHS officials who, after reviewing our analysis, identified additional sectors their assessments or assessment requirements may cover. The offices and components provided the data from their databases or other sources as shown in table 7.

---

[7]According to Coast Guard guidance implementing the MTSA requirements, regulated facilities are to receive annual compliance examinations or security spot check checks to verify the facilities are implementing security measures contained in their facility security plans. The Security and Accountability For Every Port Act of 2006 (SAFE Port Act, among other things, amended MTSA to direct the Coast Guard to inspect facility compliance with its approved facility security plan periodically, but not less than two times per year, at least one of which is to be an inspection conducted without notice to the facility. Pub. L. No. 109-347, § 103, 120 Stat. 1884, 1888 (2006). Because a MTSA-regulated facility's security plan is to include a vulnerability assessment (facility security assessment), we used these data to determine the number of facilities that were required to complete a vulnerability assessment to meet the MTSA regulatory requirements. To avoid overcounting, our analysis of this data included an adjustment for the multiple inspections and spot checks the Coast Guard is to make at a regulated facility each year so that multiple visits to the same facility were counted only once. This adjustment provided an estimate of the number of MTSA-regulated facilities that had completed a vulnerability assessment.

Table 7: Sources for Vulnerability Assessment-Related Data and Number of Records Provided, by Department of Homeland Security (DHS) Office and Component

DHS office or component	Assessment effort or requirement	Name of system or source of data provided to GAO	Number of records provided[a]
Coast Guard	Maritime Transportation Security Act-regulated facility vulnerability assessments	Maritime Information Safety and Law Enforcement (MISLE) application	17,822
	Port Security Assessments	Homeport database	93
Federal Protective Service (FPS)	Modified Infrastructure Survey Tool	FPS Gateway	1,835
Infrastructure Security Compliance Division (ISCD)	Chemical Facility Anti-Terrorism Standards Security Vulnerability Assessment	Chemical Security Management System, Chemical Security Assessment Tool, and CHEMSEC databases	1,290
Protective Security Coordination Division (PSCD)	Infrastructure Survey Tool	IP Gateway	2,469
	Site Assistance Visit	IP Gateway	786
Transportation Security Administration (TSA)	Baseline Assessment for Security Enhancements	Sharepoint	135
	Freight Rail Risk Analysis Tool	Manually maintained program records	214
	Joint Vulnerability Assessment	Sharepoint	91
	Pipeline Security Critical Facility Security Review	Manually maintained program records	122

Sources: Coast Guard, FPS, ISCD, PSCD, and TSA. | GAO-14-507

[a]We requested records of assessments that were completed or conducted during our period of analysis, fiscal year 2011 through fiscal year 2013.

To conduct our analysis, we used a Statistical Analysis System (SAS) to match the different data sets and summarize the results. Because we found that records from the various offices and components did not share common formats or identifiers that allowed us to easily match them, we had to match the data based on asset names and addresses. However, names and addresses were generally not entered in a standardized way, so we had to develop a process to standardize the available information and identify potential matches based on similar names or addresses. To prepare the data for our analysis, we did the following where necessary:

- We standardized the date formats for fields that tracked when assessments were conducted (dates across lists might have formats such as 01/01/10 or 1/1/2010 and needed to be standardized to ensure appropriate matching within certain time frames).

- We standardized state fields (across data sets, a state might be listed as Alabama or AL, for example).
- We retrieved additional data through IP Gateway on the street addresses of facilities visited by PSCD, where available, and added the data to the records provided by PSCD.[8]

After preparing the data, we used an SAS function (SPEDIS) to compare the records of different offices and components by measuring the asymmetric spelling distance between the words in records, that is, how close the words in a record are to others in how they are spelled. This function accounts for possible misspellings or various versions of the words used in the records to generate possible pairs of matching assets by determining the likelihood that names and addresses of records from different data sets match. SAS allows users to select a value of the SPEDIS function from a range of 0 to 200 to serve as a cutoff point for how closely two separate records must match in how they are spelled in order to be identified as a possible match. A value of 0 would identify only exact matches, whereas a value of 200 would identify matches with a wider range of spelling differences. Consequently, an analysis using a lower relative SPEDIS value will likely identify fewer possible matches than would a higher relative SPEDIS value analysis. Using a SPEDIS value of 30, the analysis identified 1,623 possible matches among the 10 assessment activities based on similarities in the asset names or addresses.[9]

The possible matches identified by the SAS analysis were written to an Excel spreadsheet, and were then independently reviewed by at least two analysts to determine whether the possible pairs identified by the program were a match, potential match, or not a match. This review found over 130 instances where the names and addresses of assets appeared to at least potentially match between the data sets of at least two DHS offices or components, indicating that the asset may have been assessed or was required to complete an assessment by more than one DHS office or component. However, as noted in the report, inconsistencies between the data sets prevented us from determining definitively the extent to which

---

[8]PSCD was unable to provide the street addresses of facilities it assessed as part of its data submittal and provided us with access to IP Gateway as a means to locate and retrieve the information for use in our analysis.

[9]We decided to use a value of 30 after conducting multiple preliminary analyses using higher and lower values.

the assets from one list were the same as those in another. For example, in some cases, assets seemed to be potential matches but there were differences in the assets or facility names or addresses.

In addition, we collected and analyzed documentation on NPPD, the Coast Guard, and TSA; processes; procedures; and systems for gathering, storing, sharing, and using information collected during assessments of CI. We also interviewed a mix of field-based officials with NPPD, TSA, and the Coast Guard at five selected locations to obtain information on their roles in assessing CI, the extent to which assets may have received assessment requests by multiple offices or components, and the extent to which assessments may have been canceled because of assets being previously assessed by another DHS office or component. Locations were Anchorage, Alaska; Houston, Texas; Portland, Oregon; Seattle, Washington; and Tampa, Florida, selected to provide variety in the types of CI assets assessed, and geographic location, and represent a mix of projects in IP's Regional Resiliency Assessment Program (RRAP).[10] We also interviewed an official of a national association representing CI owners and operators within 1 of the 16 sectors to obtain information on their perspectives on DHS's CI vulnerability assessment activities. Interviews with these officials cannot be generalized to the universe of CI sectors and locations. However, when combined with the information gathered on DHS documentation and program guidance, they provide valuable insights about how the assessment efforts are being carried out in practice by the offices and components in the field, and the extent to which actions have been taken to minimize potential duplication or overlap among the various assessment activities. To understand the requirements in handling and sharing certain critical information collected during some assessments—information designated as Protected Critical Infrastructure Information

---

[10]The RRAP was developed in 2009 by DHS's NPPD IP and is an analysis of infrastructure clusters and systems in specific geographic areas or regions, examining vulnerabilities, threats, and potential consequences to identify, among other things, dependencies and interdependencies among participating assets. RRAP projects are conducted by DHS officials in collaboration with other federal officials; state, local, territorial, and tribal officials; and the private sector depending upon the sectors and assets selected. Between fiscal years 2009 and 2012, DHS conducted 27 RRAP projects in various locations throughout the country.

(PCII)—we interviewed officials in DHS's PCII Program office and reviewed documentation on PCII regulations and requirements.[11]

To address our third objective, on the extent to which DHS is positioned to manage an integrated and coordinated government-wide approach for vulnerability assessment activities, we reviewed documentation and interviewed PSCD, TSA, and Coast Guard headquarters- and field-based officials about working with SSAs to conduct their assessment activities.[12] We reviewed documentation and interviewed officials at federal agencies external to DHS with SSA or sector regulatory responsibilities (Departments of Agriculture, Defense, Energy, Health and Human Services, Transportation, and Treasury; Environmental Protection Agency; Federal Energy Regulatory Commission; Food and Drug Administration; General Services Administration; and the Nuclear Regulatory Commission) to inventory their assessment tools and methods. We compared this inventory against one that DHS IP provided of the assessment tools and methods it was aware SSAs and other federal agencies external to DHS were providing. We focused on the tools and methods that DHS and the SSAs and other federal agencies external to DHS identified as currently being offered or under way within their respective sectors during the period of our review and did not include other tools and methods that were previously offered or required but are no longer such as those to meet the requirements of the Public Health Security and Bioterrorism Preparedness and Response Act of 2002.[13] Because our scope focused on those tools and methods identified

---

[11]In general, PCII is validated Critical Infrastructure Information (CII)—that is, information not customarily in the public domain and related to the security of critical infrastructure or protected systems—that is voluntarily submitted, directly or indirectly, to DHS for its use regarding the security of critical infrastructure and protected systems, analysis, warning, interdependency study, recovery, reconstitution, or other appropriate purpose. See 6 C.F.R. § 29.2(b), (g). Pursuant to the Critical Infrastructure Information Act of 2002, DHS established the PCII Program to institute a means to facilitate the voluntary sharing of critical infrastructure information with the federal government by providing assurances of safeguarding and limited disclosure. See 6 U.S.C. §§ 131-34; see also 6 C.F.R. pt. 29 (implementing the CII Act through the establishment of uniform procedures for the receipt, care, and storage of voluntarily submitted CII). DHS has established a PCII Program Office, which is responsible for, among other things, validating information provided by CI partners as PCII and developing protocols to access and safeguard all that is deemed PCII.

[12]See app. I for a list of the sectors and their respective SSAs.

[13]See Pub. L. No. 107-188, 116 Stat. 594.

by DHS and the SSAs and other federal agencies external to DHS, the list we identified through our work is not necessarily exhaustive, and there may be additional tools and methods offered by others that we did not capture as part of our work. However, this information provided insights as to the extent to which assessment tools and methods were being offered or provided by other agencies and departments external to DHS. We also reviewed a selected sample of assessment tools provided by SSAs and compared their contents against the key areas of vulnerability assessments covered by DHS offices and components. The SSA tools were selected because they (1) were web-based and readily accessible and (2) provided illustrative examples of the similarities and differences between assessments offered by DHS and sectors external to DHS that also sponsor assessment tools. We then compared the results of these steps against federal internal control standards.[14]

We conducted this performance audit from April 2013 to September 2014 in accordance with generally accepted government auditing standards. Those standards require that we plan and perform the audit to obtain sufficient, appropriate evidence to provide a reasonable basis for our findings and conclusions based on our audit objectives. We believe that the evidence obtained provides a reasonable basis for our findings and conclusions based on our audit objectives.

---

[14]GAO, *Standards for Internal Control in the Federal Government*, GAO/AIMD-00-21.3.1 (Washington, D.C.: Nov. 1, 1999). Internal control is an integral component of an organization's management that provides reasonable assurance that the following objectives are being achieved: effectiveness and efficiency of operations, reliability of financial reporting, and compliance with applicable laws and regulations. These standards, issued pursuant to the requirements of the Federal Managers' Financial Integrity Act of 1982 (FMFIA), provide the overall framework for establishing and maintaining internal control in the federal government.

Appendix IV: Selected Areas Included or Considered in Vulnerability Assessment Tools and Methods

This appendix describes selected areas of vulnerability assessed by various tools and methods used by Department of Homeland Security (DHS) offices and components. We obtained definitions of these areas through various DHS assessment templates and guidance documents, such as the National Infrastructure Protection Plan (NIPP), NIPP Supplemental Tools (e.g., Supplemental Tool: National Protection and Programs Directorate Resources to Support Vulnerability Assessments and tools identified within this document), and the *DHS Risk Lexicon*, among others.[1] Table 8 shows selected areas identified in various DHS assessment templates and guidance. However, as discussed in the report, DHS vulnerability assessments we reviewed did not consistently address all areas.

---

[1]DHS, Risk Steering Committee, *DHS Risk Lexicon* (Washington, D.C.: September 2010). DHS developed the risk lexicon to provide a common set of official terms and definitions to ease and improve the communication of risk-related issues for DHS and its partners.

Table 8: Selected Areas Included or Considered in Vulnerability Assessment Tools or Methods

Vulnerabilities to intentional acts – vulnerability assessment identifies mitigation measures in place to address acts intended to disrupt or destroy critical infrastructure (CI), such as acts of terrorism.

Vulnerabilities to all-hazards – vulnerability assessment identifies mitigation measures in place to address acts from intended, accidental, or naturally occurring hazards, such as acts of terrorism and accidental incidents and floods, hurricanes, earthquakes, or tsunamis.

Resilience management – assessment identifies actions taken by the CI to ensure collaboration/coordination of resilience-related activities (i.e., business continuity, emergency management, or security management) that can keep the CI functioning after disruptive events such as natural disasters, terrorism, crime, and computer and human error.

Security force – assessment identifies whether a facility has a security force (individuals with unique and sole duties to provide security), and staffing, equipment/weapons, and training related to security force efforts.

Perimeter security – assessment identifies perimeter security measures in place, such as fences, gates, vehicle access control, patrols, barriers, or asset hardening.

Entry controls – assessment identifies entry controls in place during operating and nonoperating hours; the types of individuals allowed into the facility; and the level of access granted to these individuals, such as employees, visitors (if allowed), contractors/vendors and customers/patrons/the public.

Electronic security systems – assessment identifies if CI uses a security system such as an intrusion detection system or closed-circuit television (CCTV), among others.

Utility systems/ providers/dependencies identified – assessment identifies whether CI supports the function of a region by providing essential resources used by other CI, government entities, or the population, or are dependent on others. Dependencies are the linkages between CI – the reliance of a facility or system on a specific facility, system, or resource to carry out its core operations.

Cybersecurity – an assessment of cybersecurity involves auditing the systems, policies, and procedures within an organization to identify critical systems, and identifies, in general terms, incidents that could violate written or implied security policies, such as phishing scams, stolen data, denial-of-service attacks, or other disruptions, and whether the facility utilizes formal, external cybersecurity guidance and standards for identifying and implementing cybersecurity controls (management, operational, or technical) (e.g. National Institute of Standards and Technology Special Publications 800-series).

Inventory controls/measures – if applicable, assessment identifies if a facility has a formal control or procedure to determine what inventory is in place, and who has access, such as a measure to determine who has keys to critical areas or inventory, or measures used at the facility that would help reduce vulnerability to theft/diversion like automated, regularly occurring electronic inventory accounting.

Source: GAO analysis of Department of Homeland Security vulnerability assessment templates and guidance. | GAO-14-507

Appendix V: Examples of Assessment Tools and Methods offered by Agencies External to the Department of Homeland Security

This appendix describes vulnerability assessment tools and methods offered by sector-specific agencies (SSA) and federal agencies external to DHS. Table 9 shows the SSA or other federal agency, the tool or method, and a description of the tool or method. As discussed in the report, other tools and methods are also offered by these agencies, but the examples included in table 9 provide insights into the types of tools and methods offered or conducted by SSAs and federal agencies in addition to those offered by various DHS offices and components.

Table 9: Examples of Vulnerability Assessment Tools and Methods Offered by Sector-Specific Agencies (SSA) and Federal Agencies External to the Department of Homeland Security (DHS)

Agency	Name of tool or method	Description of tool or method
Environmental Protection Agency (EPA)	Vulnerability Self-Assessment Tool (VSAT)	VSAT is a risk assessment software tool for water, wastewater, and combined utilities of all sizes to assist owners and operators in performing security threats and natural hazards risk assessments, among other things.
	Climate Resilience Evaluation and Awareness Tool (CREAT)	CREAT is a self-assessment tool that allows users to evaluate potential impacts of climate change on their utilities and to evaluate adaptation options to address these impacts using both traditional risk assessment and scenario-based decision making. CREAT includes a database of drinking water and wastewater utility assets (e.g., water resources, treatment plants, and pump stations) that could be affected by climate change, possible climate change-related threats (e.g., flooding, drought, or water quality), and adaptive measures that can be implemented to reduce the impacts of climate change. The tool guides users through identifying threats based on regional differences in climate change projections and designing adaptation plans based on the types of threats being considered. Following assessment, CREAT provides a series of risk reduction and cost reports that will allow the user to evaluate various adaptation options as part of long-term planning.
Federal Energy Regulatory Commission (FERC)	Dam Assessment Matrix for Security and Vulnerability Risk (DAMSVR)	DAMSVR is a vulnerability assessment methodology for dams developed by FERC in association with state dam safety officials. It is one tool that can be used to meet FERC regulatory requirements. FERC requires owners and operators of the higher criticality-ranked dam facilities to complete a vulnerability assessment of their facility and update it periodically.[a]

Appendix V: Examples of Assessment Tools
and Methods offered by Agencies External to
the Department of Homeland Security

Agency	Name of tool or method	Description of tool or method
U.S. Department of Health and Human Services (HHS), Food and Drug Administration (FDA), and the U.S. Department of Agriculture (USDA)	Vulnerability Assessment Software Tool	The Vulnerability Assessment Software Tool uses the CARVER + Shock methodology to identify areas that may be vulnerable to an attacker. CARVER is an acronym for the following six attributes used to evaluate the attractiveness of a target for attack: • Criticality – measure of public health and economic impacts of an attack • Accessibility – ability to physically access and egress from target • Recuperability – ability of system to recover from an attack • Vulnerability – ease of accomplishing attack • Effect – amount of direct loss from an attack as measured by loss in production • Recognizability – ease of identifying a target • A seventh attribute, Shock, has been added to the original six to assess the combined health, economic, and psychological impacts of an attack within the food industry.
Department of Energy (DOE)-National Nuclear Security Administration (NNSA)	Radiological Voluntary Security Enhancements	Under this program, security experts from DOE's national laboratories, led by NNSA staff, provide security assessments, share observations, and make recommendations for enhancing security at facilities that house high-risk radioactive sources. When appropriate, NNSA pays for the installation of agreed-upon security enhancements.
	Research and Test Reactors Voluntary Security Enhancement Program	NNSA conducts site visits and makes recommendations for voluntary security enhancements at research and test reactors. Security enhancements are jointly determined by NNSA and the facility owner and operator and are funded by NNSA. The voluntary enhancements complement Nuclear Regulatory Commission and Agreement State increased controls requirements. Typical security enhancements include automated access control, motion sensors, radiation sensors, electronic seals, alarm control and display systems, remote monitoring to off-site response locations, enhanced guard force communications and protection equipment, delay elements, and transportation security enhancements.
DOE- Sandia National Laboratories	Adversary Time Line Analysis System (ATLAS)	ATLAS is a software-based program used to compute the most vulnerable paths for both outsider adversary and violent insider attacks for nuclear power plants.
	Risk Assessment Methodology for Critical Infrastructures (RAM-CI)	RAM-CI uses a basic security risk assessment framework common to all critical infrastructures and can be adapted to any critical infrastructure sector. Risk is a function of T (threat), V (vulnerability) and C (consequences). The RAM-CI tool is designed to evaluate and estimate T, V, and C for any given asset and threat.
	Risk Assessment Methodology for Water Utilities (RAM-W)	RAM-W was designed to assist water utilities in assessing risks from malevolent threats. A prioritized plan for consequence mitigation, security upgrades, modifications to operational procedures, or policy changes can be developed to mitigate identified risks.

Source: GAO analysis of EPA, DHS, DOE, FERC, HHS, and USDA documents. | GAO-14-507

[a]These requirements are laid out in the FERC Security Program for Hydropower Projects. According to these requirements, owners of higher-criticality dams (Security Group 1 dams) are to update their vulnerability assessments annually and redo them every 5 years.

Appendix VI: Comments from the Department of Homeland Security

U.S. Department of Homeland Security
Washington, DC 20528

Homeland Security

September 3, 2014

Stephen L. Caldwell
Director, Homeland Security and Justice Issues
U.S. Government Accountability Office
441 G Street NW
Washington, DC 20548

Re: Draft Report GAO-14-507, "CRITICAL INFRASTRUCTURE PROTECTION: DHS Action Needed to Enhance Integration and Coordination of Vulnerability Assessment Efforts"

Dear Mr. Caldwell:

Thank you for the opportunity to review and comment on this draft report. The U.S. Department of Homeland Security (DHS) appreciates the U.S. Government Accountability Office's (GAO's) work in planning and conducting its review and issuing this report.

DHS is pleased to note GAO's positive recognition that the Department has taken actions to assess vulnerabilities at Critical Infrastructure (CI) facilities and within groups of related infrastructure, regions, and systems; including conducting or requiring thousands of vulnerability assessments. DHS agrees that greater ability to share data and leverage multiple data sets would better serve the CI community. DHS has made significant progress in integrating its vulnerability assessments, recognizing that this work is part of a larger effort that must be managed within the available resources for these programs.

DHS shares GAO's desire to achieve as much commonality and integration as practical across all CI vulnerability assessments and remains committed to working towards that end with its interagency partners. It is important to note, however, that DHS has responsibility for 10 of the 16 CI sectors as the Sector Specific Agency (SSA). DHS, through its National Protection and Programs Directorate (NPPD), will work to implement GAO's recommendations for those 10 SSAs and will partner to assist other agencies to achieve a coordinated and common approach throughout the federal CI community.

The draft report contained six recommendations with which the Department concurs. Specifically, GAO recommended that the Secretary of Homeland Security direct the Under Secretary for NPPD work with other DHS offices and components to:

Recommendation 1: Review DHS's vulnerability assessments to identify the most important areas to be assessed, consistent with [Presidential Policy Directive] PPD-21 and the [National Infrastructure Protection Plan] NIPP, and determine the areas and level of detail that are necessary for DHS to integrate assessments and enable comparisons, and establish guidance for

DHS offices and components to ensure that these areas and level of detail are included, as appropriate, in their assessments.

Response: Concur. NPPD's Office of Infrastructure Protection (IP) has established a single system to provide the CI community with an integrated capability and consistent methodology for assessing risk to CI at all levels of government. In addition, the 2013 NIPP included two supplemental guides related to conducting assessments, "Resources to Support Vulnerability Assessments" and "Executing a Critical Infrastructure Risk Management Approach." These initiatives will be built upon to assess common elements of vulnerability assessments and develop additional guidance for DHS components.

DHS shares the goal of achieving maximum efficiency in its use of assessments and desires a data set that can be shared by all DHS components addressing critical infrastructure risks. Integration of assessments and data will include common elements but also necessary flexibility and adaptability to allow for additional data capture and analysis to meet component requirements for the assessments. DHS will convene components to plan for this review and subsequent guidance development. Guidance development and issuances will be dependent upon the initial review with consideration towards resource and budget constraints. Estimated Completion Date (ECD): June 30, 2015.

Recommendation 2: Develop an approach to ensure that vulnerability data gathered on CI assets and systems are consistently collected and maintained across DHS to facilitate the identification of potential duplication and gaps in CI coverage.

Response: Concur. The National Security Council has established a sub-Interagency Policy Committee (sub-IPC) to focus on CI data and information sharing that is taking initial steps to identify what appropriate policies and or guidance are needed to support the identification of critical information that could be shared across the infrastructure protection community. Recommendations and guidance from the sub-IPC are anticipated this calendar year. This guidance will provide appropriate departments and agencies with a common approach to CI data and information sharing which will enable access to those data elements and information necessary to support mission requirements.

Additionally, NPPD's IP has implemented a single assessment methodology with a strategic integrated approach to its own vulnerabilities and security surveys. This assessment methodology has already been implemented across multiple physical and cyber assessment tools. This scalable methodology uses an established set of core questions and answers to support consistent data collection and enable robust analytics and data comparison between physical and cyber security and resilience information collected from a variety of NPPD tools. ECD: June 30, 2015.

2

Recommendation 3: Develop and implement ways that DHS can facilitate data sharing and coordination of vulnerability assessments to minimize the risk of potential duplication or gaps in coverage.

Response: Concur. Information systems play a vital role in allowing federal, state, local, tribal, territorial, and private sector partners to identify, analyze, and manage risk to protect the Nation. As an example of how DHS is working to facilitate data sharing and coordination of vulnerability assessments, NPPD's IP has developed a secure, trusted system with supporting applications for the CI community via a secure portal, the IP Gateway, which serves as the single interface through which DHS mission partners can access tools, capabilities, and information to conduct comprehensive vulnerability assessments, risk analysis, and event and incident planning.

The IP Gateway provides various data collection, analysis, and response tools in one integrated system, streamlining access to IP's tools and datasets by leveraging a single user registration, management, and authentication process. This single assessment methodology, with a strategic integrated approach, will enable the State, Local, Tribal, and Territorial community and IP to share, compare, and identify which facilities have been assessed. Additionally, it will direct access to those assessments through the IP Gateway to reduce the burden on CI owners and operators.

NPPD IP is in the early planning stages of the next phase of the single assessment methodology which will provide a strategic integrated approach that includes IP Gateway assess to SSAs and other mission partners across DHS and the federal government, consistent with law and regulatory requirements. DHS will convene stakeholders across the Department to assess current data collection efforts, and development and implementation of coordination plans dependent on initial assessments. ECD: March 31, 2015.

GAO also recommended that the Secretary of Homeland Security direct the Under Secretary for NPPD work with SSAs and other federal agencies that have CI security responsibilities to:

Recommendation 4: Identify key CI security-related assessment tools and methods used or offered by SSAs and other federal agencies.

Response: Concur. NPPD IP will lead an inventory survey on the security-related assessment tools and methods used by the 16 SSAs for the purposes of assessing CI vulnerabilities. The survey will leverage existing information as reported through Sector-Specific Plans and the National Annual Report data call. ECD: August 31, 2015.

Recommendation 5: Analyze the key CI security-related assessment tools and methods offered by SSAs and other federal agencies to determine the areas they capture.

Response: Concur. NPPD IP will use the inventory data captured as a result of implementing Recommendation 4 to assess methodologies and areas covered by each tool. ECD: To Be Determined.

3

Recommendation 6: Develop and provide guidance for what areas should be included in
vulnerability assessments of CI that can be used by DHS, SSAs, and other CI partners in an
integrated and coordinated manner, among and across sectors, where appropriate.

Response: Concur. While DHS does not have authority to require inclusion of specific
characteristics in vulnerability assessments conducted by other departments and agencies, DHS
can and does work to promote consistency across assessments in order to ensure that data is
comparable. The NIPP 2013 includes the "Supplemental Tool: Implementing a Risk
Management Approach," which provides foundational guidance regarding how to understand
risk as it relates to CI. This document establishes shared definitions and a broad framework for
understanding vulnerability assessments as a component of an overarching risk management
system. DHS can continue to refine this guidance, as necessary, recognizing that the details of
individual vulnerability assessments will necessarily vary depending on the nature of each sector
and regulatory requirements. ECD: June 30, 2015.

Again, thank you for the opportunity to review and comment on this draft report. Technical
comments were previously provided under separate cover. Please feel free to contact me if you
have any questions. We look forward to working with you in the future.

Sincerely,

Jim H. Crumpacker, CIA, CFE
Director
Departmental GAO/OIG Liaison Office

4

Appendix VII: Comments from the Department of Energy

Department of Energy
Washington, DC 20585

August 28, 2014

Mr. Stephen L. Caldwell
Director
Homeland Security and Justice Issues
U.S. Government Accountability Office
Washington, DC 20548

Dear Director Caldwell:

The Department of Energy (DOE) appreciates the opportunity to respond to the Government Accountability Office's (GAO) Report, "Critical Infrastructure Protection: DHS Action Needed to Enhance Integration and Coordination of Vulnerability Assessment Efforts."

General Comments:

- The report states that there should be a single government-wide approach to assessments; however, in our view, the energy sector has its own vulnerabilities, risk acceptance tolerance and threat mitigation methods and therefore, a "one size fits all" may not make sense. Ultimately some flexibility must be built in to assessing the critical infrastructure (CI). In addition, there are costs to both the government and the asset owners in developing, maintaining and managing a very large database as identified in the report.

- There is a focus on information sharing "department-wide" for DHS, but this ignores the need for information sharing between DHS and the SSAs that work directly with sector asset owner/operators. Assessments in the energy sector, for example, should be coordinated with the SSA (DOE), and all relevant data that is used by DHS should be shared with DOE at the conclusion of any engagements involving industry.

- The report, which is DHS-focused, provides almost no attention to private sector vulnerability assessments being undertaken both by individual asset owners and operators as well as the numerous private companies offering assessment methodologies and services to asset owners. If GAO took these perspectives into account, they would have a more complete picture of threat assessment and mitigation approaches.

 Printed with soy ink on recycled paper

Detailed Comments:

- The report is missing references to a popular tool being used in the energy sector: the Cybersecurity Capability Maturity Model (C2M2), which is dual-logoed by both DOE and DHS. The tool was developed by industry, in collaboration with the federal government, academia, and the national labs. More information can be found here: http://energy.gov/oe/services/cybersecurity/cybersecurity-capability-maturity-model-c2m2-program. U.S. Coast Guard has recently discussed adapting the C2M2 for their purposes.

- Likewise, in terms of cybersecurity, there is no mention of the recent DHS and Sector-Specific Agency (SSA) efforts surrounding the NIST Cybersecurity Framework from EO 13636, which is supposed to capture the similarities and functions/categories needed for CI cybersecurity across all 16 sectors.

- The DHS Cyber Resilience Review (CRR) is also missing from the discussion of tools used by DHS for cybersecurity. The CRR collects data from CI asset owner/operators across all 16 critical infrastructure sectors.

- In Table 5 "energy" and "government facilities" are the only CI sectors in which all five DHS offices or components are selected. The table and accompanying text should have more discussion, particularly on the overlap concerning the energy sector, to explain the nature of the vulnerability assessments so as to facilitate comparison to assessments conducted by the energy SSA and others.

Thank you again for the opportunity to provide comment on the draft report. We look forward to receiving your final report.

Sincerely,

Patricia A. Hoffman
Assistant Secretary
Office of Electricity Delivery and Energy Reliability
U.S. Department of Energy

Appendix VIII: Comments from the Nuclear Regulatory Commission

UNITED STATES
NUCLEAR REGULATORY COMMISSION
WASHINGTON, D.C. 20555-0001

August 28, 2014

Mr. Stephen Caldwell
Director, Homeland Security
 and Justice Issues
U.S. Government and Accountability Office
Washington, DC 20548

Dear Mr. Caldwell:

Thank you for giving the U.S. Nuclear Regulatory Commission (NRC) the opportunity to review and comment on the U.S. Government Accountability Office's draft report GAO-14-507, "Critical Infrastructure Protection: DHS [Department of Homeland Security] Action Needed to Enhance Integration and Coordination of Vulnerability Assessment Efforts." The NRC has reviewed the report and would like to provide a single comment.

There is an erroneous reference to NRC in Table 6 on page 35. In particular, the table indicates that the NRC "offers" the Vulnerability Integrated Security Assessment (VISA) methodology tool. Footnote d of the table explains that DHS identified the NRC as providing the tool, but notes that the NRC did not identify the tool as one it developed or provided to its licensees.

The NRC did not develop the VISA methodology tool. Based on NRC staff research, the VISA methodology appears to have been developed by Science Applications International Corporation (SAIC) in the 1970s. The staff identified references as early as 1977 to SAIC publications and presentations at professional society meetings on the VISA methodology. Over the next 20 years, SAIC made enhancements to the methodology and identified additional uses for the methodology. Since then, many other companies as well as government agencies have taken advantage of the VISA methodology.

The NRC does not provide the VISA methodology tool to its licensees. The NRC developed NUREG/CR-7145, "Nuclear Power Plant Security Assessment Guide," to provide guidance to NRC licensees on how they might conduct a security self-assessment. NUREG/CR-7145 identifies the VISA methodology as one methodology, amongst others, that licensees might consider for use in conducting these security assessments. Neither the NUREG nor NRC regulations require that NRC licensees use the VISA methodology tool.

S. Caldwell   -2-

DHS has incorrectly identified the NRC as providing the VISA methodology tool to its licensees. The NRC requests that Footnote d to Table 6 be revised to indicate that VISA is a privately-developed tool that is referenced in NRC guidance as an acceptable method by which to conduct security self-assessments, but that the NRC does not require its use, and does not provide the tool to any licensee or other entity in the nuclear sector.

Sincerely,

Mark A. Satorius
Executive Director
 for Operations

Appendix IX: GAO Contact and Staff Acknowledgments

GAO Contact	Stephen L. Caldwell, (202) 512-8777 or caldwells@gao.gov
Staff Acknowledgments	In addition to the contact named above, John F. Mortin, Assistant Director, and Christopher Hatscher, Analyst-in-Charge, managed this assignment. Chuck Bausell, Orlando Copeland, Andrew M. Curry, Michele C. Fejfar, Eric D. Hauswirth, Mitch Karpman, Tracey King, Jessica Orr, and Katrina D. Taylor made significant contributions to the work.

Related GAO Products

Critical Infrastructure Protection: DHS Could Strengthen the Management of the Regional Resiliency Assessment Program. GAO-13-616. Washington, D.C.: July 30, 2013.

Critical Infrastructure Protection: DHS List of Priority Assets Needs to Be Validated and Reported to Congress. GAO-13-296. Washington, D.C.: March 25, 2013.

Critical Infrastructure Protection: Preliminary Observations on DHS Efforts to Assess Chemical Security Risk and Gather Feedback on Facility Outreach. GAO-13-412T. Washington, D.C.: March 14, 2013.

Critical Infrastructure Protection: An Implementation Strategy Could Advance DHS's Coordination of Resilience Efforts across Ports and Other Infrastructure. GAO-13-11. Washington, D.C.: October 25, 2012.

Critical Infrastructure Protection: Summary of DHS Actions to Better Manage Its Chemical Security Program. GAO-12-1044T. Washington, D.C.: September 20, 2012.

Critical Infrastructure Protection: DHS Is Taking Action to Better Manage Its Chemical Security Program, but It Is Too Early to Assess Results. GAO-12-567T. Washington, D.C.: September 11, 2012.

Critical Infrastructure: DHS Needs to Refocus Its Efforts to Lead the Government Facilities Sector. GAO-12-852. Washington, D.C.: August 13, 2012.

Critical Infrastructure Protection: DHS Is Taking Action to Better Manage Its Chemical Security Program, but It Is Too Early to Assess Results. GAO-12-515T. Washington, D.C.: July 26, 2012.

Critical Infrastructure Protection: DHS Could Better Manage Security Surveys and Vulnerability Assessments. GAO-12-378. Washington, D.C.: May 31, 2012.

Critical Infrastructure Protection: DHS Has Taken Action Designed to Identify and Address Overlaps and Gaps in Critical Infrastructure Security Activities. GAO-11-537R. Washington, D.C.: May 19, 2011.

Critical Infrastructure Protection: DHS Efforts to Assess and Promote Resiliency Are Evolving but Program Management Could Be Strengthened. GAO-10-772. Washington, D.C.: September 23, 2010.

Critical Infrastructure Protection: Update to National Infrastructure Protection Plan Includes Increased Emphasis on Risk Management and Resilience. GAO-10-296. Washington, D.C.: March 5, 2010.

The Department of Homeland Security's (DHS) Critical Infrastructure Protection Cost-Benefit Report. GAO-09-654R. Washington, D.C.: June 26, 2009.

Information Technology: Federal Laws, Regulations, and Mandatory Standards to Securing Private Sector Information Technology Systems and Data in Critical Infrastructure Sectors. GAO-08-1075R. Washington, D.C.: September 16, 2008.

Risk Management: Strengthening the Use of Risk Management Principles in Homeland Security. GAO-08-904T. Washington, D.C.: June 25, 2008.

Critical Infrastructure: Sector Plans Complete and Sector Councils Evolving. GAO-07-1075T. Washington, D.C.: July 12, 2007.

Critical Infrastructure Protection: Sector Plans and Sector Councils Continue to Evolve. GAO-07-706R. Washington, D.C.: July 10, 2007.

Critical Infrastructure: Challenges Remain in Protecting Key Sectors. GAO-07-626T. Washington, D.C.: March 20, 2007.

Homeland Security: Progress Has Been Made to Address the Vulnerabilities Exposed by 9/11, but Continued Federal Action Is Needed to Further Mitigate Security Risks. GAO-07-375. Washington, D.C.: January 24, 2007.

Critical Infrastructure Protection: Progress Coordinating Government and Private Sector Efforts Varies by Sectors' Characteristics. GAO-07-39. Washington, D.C.: October 16, 2006.

Information Sharing: DHS Should Take Steps to Encourage More Widespread Use of Its Program to Protect and Share Critical Infrastructure Information. GAO-06-383. Washington, D.C.: April 17, 2006.

Risk Management: Further Refinements Needed to Assess Risks and Prioritize Protective Measures at Ports and Other Critical Infrastructure. GAO-06-91. Washington, D.C.: December 15, 2005.

Please Print on Recycled Paper.